HEADLINING
SOCIOLOGY

Second Edition

Patricia Gray

Holt, Rinehart and Winston of Canada, Limited

Canadian Cataloguing in Publication Data
Gray, Patricia, 1935-
    Headlining sociology

Includes index.
ISBN 0-03-921875-9

1. Sociology. 2. Sociology – Problems, exercises, etc.
I. Title.

HM73.G72 1985   301   C85-098586-2

Publisher: Anthony Luengo
Developmental Editor: Tessa McWatt
Copy Editor: Francine Geraci
Production Manager: Anna Kress
Cover: Michael van Elsen Design Inc.
Interior Design: Maher & Murtagh
Typesetting: Parker Typesetting

Printed in Canada

  2 3 4 5 91 90 89

Preface

Headlining Sociology contains over fifty articles from Canadian newspapers and magazines with questions related to each article. The articles are grouped into twenty sections. They have been chosen to illustrate the topics and concepts usually covered in an introductory sociology course. They provide real-world cases for sociological analysis either through class discussion or written answers to the questions. There are an additional twenty assignments in which students have to find their own illustrative clipping.

Students find applying what they learn both helpful and stimulating. This process is especially useful for those who study sociology as part of their training in other areas (such as journalism, nursing, education or business). Using this workbook may also encourage those who do not normally read newspapers and news magazines to do so, thereby increasing their knowledge and interest in current events.

Objectives

The first objective in *Headlining Sociology* is to stimulate students' interest by showing them ways in which sociological analysis can be used to evaluate and understand the situations reported in the print media. By engaging in this process students will also learn how to apply sociological insights in assessing events in their own lives.

The second objective is to help students to understand and review the sociological theories, concepts, and issues discussed in their lectures and main texts. A written analysis or classroom discussion of the situations portrayed in each article will enhance students' abilities to recall and articulate the meaning of ideas that are central to the discipline of sociology.

Finally, continuous experience in analysing newspaper and magazine articles will make students more discriminating in evaluating these as sources of information, and in identifying the bias of reporters or publishers.

Newspapers and magazines as a source of articles

Newspapers and magazine articles are a familiar and important source of information and entertainment. Using them for the assignments in this book involves a new way of looking at press reports. Students are asked to apply sociological analysis to the material contained in the articles and also to assess the content, impact and biases of the newspaper or magazine article.

Journalists have strict professional standards, and newspaper publishers have a sense of social responsibility and a desire to present full and balanced reports. But there are pressures on the publishers of newspapers and magazines—pressures that introduce biases and distortions into the selection of the news items that will be reported, into the attention given to issues, and into the actual reporting of events. The following considerations should be kept in mind when reading the press, and in following any of the other mass media as well.

The media have to exist within and are part of the economic system. Most are run with the aim of making a profit for their owners. As media revenues are derived primarily from advertising, and advertising revenues in turn are dependent on circulation figures, publishers are concerned about circulation. To maintain profits publishers must avoid offending their readers or advertisers. Consequently, newspaper writers tend to conform to mainstream social values and support conventional social views. They are critical of people and incidents that threaten or violate these values.

In addition, to capture attention and increase readership, events are frequently reported in a sensational way. Editors and reporters tend to select items that will shock, electrify, and entertain, as well as inform. The emphasis is therefore on brevity, readability and simple, often colloquial, language. Topical issues are reported daily until it is thought readers are no longer following the issues, at which point they are dropped for something new.

Cost constraints on reporting, as well as notions about reader attention spans, frequently prevent in-depth analysis of complex or many-sided issues. Local issues may not be fully or accurately reported since local reporters often do not have the time or the expertise to cover all sides of the issue fully. National and international news items usually come from wire service reports and these are usually brief, written to satisfy a wide range of newspapers, and written to facilitate even further cutting if necessary.

This book should serve to heighten awareness of the fact that most of the information we receive, from the media and from other sources, is incomplete and possibly biased or distorted. The ability to uncover the assumptions and the implicit values underlying any argument or presentation is essential if we presume ever to be able to assess realistically the information we encounter, whether it be print or electronic, public or private.

To the student

Sociology involves attempting to understand society, social organizations, our social life and relationships with others from a social perspective. This book is designed to help you to take a new look at some of the issues in Canadian society, and provide new insights into some of the apparently simple everyday occurrences that you previously took for granted.

Introductory sociology courses are intended to be an overview of the field of sociology. As a student, you should aim to gain a knowledge of the basic concepts and theoretical perspectives of the subject. Furthermore, you should develop the skill of using these ideas to analyse your own experience as well as events and issues in Canada and elsewhere.

Concepts provide a means of generalizing about such social phenomena as primary groups, social class, socialization, deviant acts, norms and so forth. These concepts simplify and identify the key properties common to a number of cases. They label the special characteristics of these phenomena and make discussion, comparison, and analysis possible. Finding and using examples, as you are asked to do in this book, helps to clarify the concepts and strengthens your understanding of their meaning.

Since sociologists do not agree on one explanation of the workings of society, most sociology courses will acquaint you with a variety of interpretations of how society is organized, and how people can live together. You will have to decide on the merits and applicability of any one of these interpretations in a particular situation under analysis. In sociology these various interpretations of the way society works are called *theoretical perspectives*. A theoretical perspective can colloquially be called a general world view; the specific underlying assumptions of each perspective provide a particular orientation or view of the social world as well as a broad framework for empirical inquiry. A brief summary of the major theoretical perspectives is given in the introduction to Section 1.

In analysing an article, first read the introduction, then the article and the questions, carefully. The introductions to the sections and the articles are intended as a supplement to your course material; they should help you to focus your thoughts when reading the article and relating the questions to it. You should also review the appropriate sections in your lecture notes, textbook, and other course material before you begin. Concepts to consider in answering the questions are listed for each article. Not all of them need to be used in your analysis,

and you should not hesitate to introduce other concepts and ideas you think are relevant.

The questions associated with each article are designed to bring together the concepts and ideas learned in your course, your general knowledge, and the content of the article. Some of the questions will test your ability to abstract material from the articles. The ability to catalogue material mentally as you read is a useful skill to acquire and comes with practice.

If you are preparing for a class discussion, you should outline the answer to each question so that you can present your main point and supporting arguments clearly and concisely. If you are writing answers, you should keep them short; though it is far easier to write at length than to write a short paragraph that incorporates the main points and says exactly what you intend, you should aim at clear, precise writing. Developing this skill takes practice.

To the instructor

Headlining Sociology is not a textbook. Depending on how you develop the course, *Headlining Sociology* can be used in conjunction with your own notes and handouts, lectures, or as an applied supplement to a textbook. *Headlining Sociology* contains two types of assignments: fifty sets of questions based on the articles provided, and twenty additional assignments in which students are directed to find a clipping on a given topic and analyse it according to the instructions given.

In order to provide flexibility, the assignments are grouped into twenty sections, and can be selected and used in any order, depending on what is most suitable for the course.

Each article has a short introduction that provides background information where necessary and a framework for the questions. A list of concepts to consider establishes a definitional framework for the questions. The questions, in series, build on one another. They probe the student's understanding of these concepts and his or her ability to apply the key concepts in analysing the situation and issues raised in the article. Some of the questions cannot be answered directly from the article; they are included to ensure that students relate what is being discussed to the material covered in the course and to their own knowledge and experience.

The index at the back of the book lists the concepts to consider which appear at the beginning of each article. This can be used for cross-reference.

Headlining Sociology has been used in a variety of ways in the classroom. The articles and questions work well as a basis for class discussion, but it is best if the article is assigned beforehand in order to make the best use of class time. In larger classes, having the article and questions in front of them enables students to follow the discussion even if they are not inclined to participate.

One alternative in larger classes is to divide the class into smaller groups. This provides more opportunity for students to participate, and shy students may be more inclined to speak.

The purpose of the discussion is to clarify and reinforce the key concepts and to elicit as wide a variety of ideas as possible. In any discussion group, therefore, it is important to provide positive feedback to the speakers, and to emphasize that no one will be marked down or criticized for answers that are incorrect or "off base." Misunderstandings can be used to clarify answers. Class discussions are good for developing ideas and drawing out differing points of view. These discussions can also draw upon the variety of experiences students have had, given their various ethnic backgrounds, geographic origins and, perhaps, a wide range in their ages and job histories. Treating all views and opinions with respect encourages students to contribute and to benefit from seeing the diversity of outlooks.

Each of the assignments can also be used for written work. You can select appropriate ones, or the students can be instructed to choose a specific number to do during the course. The latter method ensures that students will read more of the assignments.

Some of the questions ask students to define a concept and then to apply it. The object of these questions is to teach students the importance of clarifying terms before using them. Asking them to use a given concept in an answer without first defining it often produces answers that are vague and suggest that the concept has not been clearly understood.

Some of the questions are deliberately open-ended to give scope for students to think broadly. The aim of these questions is to get students to apply what they have learned; they must therefore be allowed a little space in which to do so. They should be expected to demonstrate their grasp of sociology by relating what they have studied to their own experiences and by testing their own opinions.

In summary, working through these assignments will help students to develop their analytical skills; they have to decide what is and is not relevant and to justify their choices. Whether the answers are spoken or written, they can help students develop their ability to express themselves clearly and concisely. The answers to question are not expected to be long. When the assignments are written, students should be required to write first drafts, then edit them to produce polished and concise answers.

Note from the Publisher

This text book is a key component of your course. If you are the instructor, you probably considered a number of texts carefully before choosing this as the one that would work best for you and your students. As the publisher of this book, we have made a large investment to ensure its high quality and we appreciate your recognition of our effort and accomplishment.

If you are a student, we are confident that this text will assist you in meeting the objectives of your course. Because you will find it helpful after the course is finished, hold on to it. If you re-sell it, the authors lose royalties that are rightfully theirs. Also, they lose if you photocopy their work instead of paying for it. This will discourage them from writing another edition or other books, because the effort simply would not be worth their while. In the end, everyone loses if you re-sell or photocopy.

Since we want to hear what you think about this book, please send us the stamped reply card at the end of the text. This will help us to continue publishing high quality books for your courses.

Table of Contents

1

A Sociological Perspective

Sociology views society and social life from a distinctive vantage point. It is the scientific study of social life and social behaviour. Sociologists are interested in the totality of social life and the way in which changes in one area affect other parts of the society. They are interested in individuals as members of groups, in the ways in which the social situation affects individuals and the ways in which individuals respond and influence the social environment.

Sociologists have developed a number of interpretations of how societies are organized and how people can live together. Three perspectives commonly discussed in introductory courses are 1) structural functionalism or functionalism, 2) conflict theory, and 3) symbolic interaction. These various theoretical perspectives are based on quite different assumptions about the nature of social life. Each is summarized briefly below.

Structural functionalism emphasizes social order and endeavours to explain why, for the most part, we experience life and relations with others as predictable. Structural functionalism rests on the assumption that society tends to be a stable, integrated system in which the various parts of the system function to maintain the whole. For example, in the functionalist approach, the family system is seen as responsible for reproduction and ensuring that the young are cared for and taught how to behave in a socially acceptable way; the education system continues the task of educating and socializing the young for their place in society. All the component parts of the social system are interrelated and interdependent and contribute to the system's maintenance. Functionalists assume that members of the society agree on basic social values, and that this agreement enhances stability. New social or economic developments (such as increased specialization) in the work force or other outside influences may bring about change, but any change in one part of the system will lead to changes in other parts, so that the whole remains in equilibrium. The emphasis in this perspective is on social order and on the means by which equilibrium is maintained.

Conflict theorists start from quite different assumptions about the nature of society—that conflict, competition, tensions, and discord are always present in society and create continual pressure for change. Groups within the society compete with each other in an attempt to gain their own goals. The goals that people desire may be tangible, like wealth, or intangible, like power or prestige. These are in short supply and therefore stimulate competition between the "haves" and the "have nots," whether it be on a visible or covert level. Those who have gained control of wealth, or who hold power or prestige, seek to maintain the status quo. To a large degree, they are able to do so, since they are in positions of political and economic power. Conflict theorists would also argue that values held by the various groups in society are frequently rationalizations for the status quo.

Macro-level sociology focuses on the social system, and the parts of the society that exist independently of any single individual and are thought to have an impact on individuals' lives, such as the education system. Both structural functionalism and conflict theory are used in macro-level analysis. Micro-level sociology refers to analysis at a less abstract level; the focus is on individuals in relation to others.

Symbolic interaction focuses on the interaction between people. For this micro-perspective, sociologists examine how individuals perceive the situations they are in, view the roles they and others are playing, and modify their own behaviour in accordance with these interpretations. Social organization in this perspective is more problematic, since it is the product of negotiation and understanding among individuals and small groups. Social life is viewed as a continuous process of interpretation and reinterpretation. Ethnomethodology and exhange theory are two other theories of micro-sociology that have some commonality with symbolic interaction. Ethnomethodologists study the meaning people give to language and to events. Exchange theorists focus on behaviour and the ways people assess the costs and benefits to themselves of each interaction with others.

These differing viewpoints on how society works are hard to grasp when you are beginning in sociology. After you have completed some of the work in this workbook you will begin to gain an understanding of what is implied by taking a particular theoretical approach.

The first article in this section is humorous, but makes some serious points, and illustrates micro-level analysis. The second article and the questions following it are designed to develop your understanding of macro-level analysis.

How Social Expectations Affect Relations Between People

INTRODUCTION

Any jobs that individuals hold are ranked relative to other paid positions. The criteria for the ranking are not always clear, yet the prestige associated with jobs is widely understood, if not always accepted, by everyone.

All the positions we occupy in everyday life carry with them a set of expectations relating to dress, behaviour, and appropriate attitudes. People learn these social expectations and most of the time tend to conform to them. We may object, or rebel occasionally, but we rarely do so all the time.

Occasionally we hear about someone who is interesting because he or she is different; he or she does not do things normally, or to put it in sociological terms, he or she does not conform to the norms. As you answer the questions below, consider why the story of Larry Sautchook merits a newspaper article. Answering the questions on the article provides you with one example of how micro-level analysis can be used to analyse everyday social relationships.

Cleaning man sports a touch of class by carting out trash cans in a tuxedo

By Ann Gibbon
of The Gazette

Larry Sautchook believes in bringing a little glamor to the factory. You might even say he gives his work the white glove touch.

When he shows up for work at the very average Blouse Factory on de Gaspe Avenue twice a week to perform the very average job of cleaning and sweeping, he doesn't sport a very average cleaner's uniform.

In fact, attired in a crisp scarlet evening jacket, white pants, glossy patent leather shoes, a fresh carnation in his lapel — and a snazzy pair of white gloves — he seems more suited to serving caviar than emptying garbage cans in a factory.

That outfit is just one of the 12 fancy suits which Sautchook wears on the job.

What is behind this sartorial zaniness?

"The whole idea of dressing up is being a part of elegance," explains the 48-year-old Montreal native. "I have to counterbalance the unelegant part of my job."

Sautchook's penchant for clothes of distinction began about a year and a half ago, when, 80 pounds heavier and "very fat and very ugly," he decided his image needed changing.

Clothes cost $4,800

So he lost weight and became a regular client of Classy Formal Wear. He estimates his wardrobe has cost him about $4,800.

Sautchook accommodates his expensive fashion tastes with a work schedule that would make even a workaholic cringe.

The self-employed cleaner doesn't just work in Montreal: he commutes 2,800 miles each week between Toronto and Montreal to clean a total of 30 offices and factories.

"I work like a dog," he says. An average day involves sleeping on the train from Toronto, arriving in Montreal by early morning and finishing work by noon.

Then he heads back for Toronto later in the day.

He's been at the Blouse Factory for almost a year.

He wouldn't say how much he earns each month, although Steve

4

Tafler, manager of the Blouse Factory, says he pays him $65 per month for his biweekly visits there.

Sautchook lives alone in East York, Toronto, but because he spends so much time on the train, he believes the folks at Via Rail "should give me a postal code for the train."

"Montreal friendlier"

He says while Toronto is more lucrative, "Montreal is where my heart is."

"Toronto is very cold. I've worked there for four years and haven't made one friend. I don't dress up there; I'm a slob."

But Montreal is full of friendly, interested people, he says.

While most may dismiss him as an eccentric, he has won the hearts of the workers at the Blouse Factory.

Louise Makovsky, who helps design blouses at the factory, says a highlight of her job was last Mother's Day, when he brought each woman employee a rose. "He's very pleasant," she says. "He's so lively and funny. He's always cheerful."

"He's the friendliest person," agrees receptionist Deborah Rubinger. "I don't wonder what makes him tick. There are thousands of people with idiosyncrasies. This is just very much his personality right now."

To Sautchook, though, the elegant suits are more than a gimmick. In some ways, they're a necessity, providing him with a much-needed element in his life: attention.

"To survive my day, I need one person every 15 minutes to say hello, how are you. I need people to survive."

And while his audiences may get a kick out of the lively antics of the world's best-dressed cleaner, Sautchook, whose only relative is his mother, admits it's far from the ideal life.

"I would like someone to come along and stop me. I'm not here because I want to be here. But it's the role I'm playing now until another one comes along."

The Gazette, Montreal, Tuesday, July 24, 1984, p. A-5.

Concepts to consider:

Norms, roles, sanctions, social interaction, status, symbols, symbolic interaction.

QUESTIONS

1. Explain in everyday terms what is meant when someone is called eccentric. Try again in sociological terms. Compare the two answers.

2. Does it take courage to be eccentric? Why?

3. How are cleaners normally expected to dress and behave? Are these normal expectations "a role" in the sociological sense of the term?

4. How do other workers usually relate to cleaners? Why?

5. What part do clothes play in our assessment of other people? Is clothing a symbol?

6. What rewards does Larry Sautchook get from behaving as he does? Is this what he wants as far as you can tell from the article?

7. Could you act in an eccentric manner on your job or in one of your other roles? What would be the costs, and what would be the benefits to you?

8. What is your expected role performance as a student? In your role as a student, to what degree do you conform to the role expectations in dress and behaviour? Why?

9. Look over your answers. Does refusing to conform to what is expected make a person an individual?

10. Which of the theoretical perspectives do you consider would provide the best framework for analysing eccentric social behaviour? Explain why you answer as you do.

6

Impact of Economic and Social Change

INTRODUCTION

Analysis in sociology can take place at many levels. When sociologiosts refer to macro-level analysis they mean analysis at a higher level of abstraction, focusing, for example, on changing patterns in the economy or the education system, or the impact of technological advance. The concept of the social system captures the idea of a system of mutually dependent parts: changes in one part of the system will affect the other parts of the system.

This editorial appeared in the Opasquia Times published in The Pas, Manitoba and reflects the views of the editorial staff and perhaps also the publisher. The writer surveys the changes taking place and the problems in the economy and considers the impact that these changes have on the various parts of the social system and, ultimately, on individuals.

As you read this editorial, consider how many of the changes, trends, or problems you have experienced or have thought about in planning your own future.

Lengthening lines

By Doug Lauvstad

Recently this newspaper carried a story regarding Canadian National Railway's project to hire 700 young people and give them some job experience. CN has been much maligned for a variety of reasons but we think this effort deserves praise. If every large company took the same sort of initiative that CN did we would go a long way to resolving a few of the many problems in this country.

Perhaps one of the most pressing problems of our time is unemployment. And, even though Manitoba has a relatively low unemployment figure, there are still people without jobs. Mostly young people. Outside of Manitoba, the situation worsens. And while we hear rumblings every day that there is work to be found if the prospective employee showed enough enthusiasm and a real willingness to work, there is more to it than that. In any society we will have people reluctant to work for a variety of reasons, but many young people who are willing to work must go without employment. Why? Simply because they lack experience. Where do they get experience? By working, of course, a catch-22 situation if there ever was one.

That vicious circle has been around for a long time. However, young people are facing a new situation that stacks the deck against them even more. The world is rapidly changing. We are in the midsts of a technological revolution such as we have never seen before. It is now at the point that by the time a young person graduates from a technical course technology has made his skills obsolete.

Educators, entrepreneurs and representatives of industry and commerce all agree that traditional training programs are not meeting the needs of the employers any more. They have found that two or three years of college or university does not give a person the skills necessary to compete in the job market. Specialized and, more importantly, ongoing training is the answer.

Government training programs and job creation initiatives do have their place in the battle against unemployment. But the employers, also have a responsibility to the young people, and to themselves, to do what they can to ensure a skilled, available workforce to draw upon. Unemployment is not simply the fault of the government, as many politicians and journalists would have us believe. Unemployment is a result of a lackadaisical attitude, world economics, an unwillingness to train young people and an attitude based somewhere in the Protestant Work Ethic that fails to recognize the massive change and upheaval our society is going through. Life is not as simple as it once was. At one time dropouts got a job, high school graduates got a good job and university graduates got great jobs. But that time has passed, and the longer we hold on to those archaic traditions the longer our unemployment lines will be.

Opasquia Times, Manitoba, Friday, August 3, 1984, p. 2.

Concepts to consider:

Economy, labour market, macro-sociology, micro-sociology, social change, social fact, social patterns, social system, values.

QUESTIONS

1. To clarify the idea for yourself, explain in you own words what is meant by macro-level analysis.

2. What are the causes of unemployment amongst young workers in the opinion of this editorial writer?

3. For each cause you cite, indicate where its origins lie—in the social system or with the individual?

4. What is the "Protestant Work Ethic" mentioned in the article? Is it a social value? Would most people share this ethic?

5. What changes does the editorial writer advocate with regard to the role of industry and government in the training and employment of young people?

6. What changes in social values would be required to achieve these changes?

7. What changes in the social system or economy would be required?

8. Is this article expressing a functionalist or a conflict perspective? Explain.

FIND A CLIPPING

Find a clipping in a magazine or a newspaper that discusses people who are in difficulty, and describe their situation.

Show how the social situation they are in, or social factors affecting them contribute to their predicament. Focus particularly on the social situation as it affects them.

What social constraints make it difficult for these people to work out a solution to their problem? Is there evidence in the article of anything that will aid them in finding a solution?

2

Research Methods

Sociological research must be carefully designed and carried out as planned, otherwise it will lead to results that are inconclusive or ambiguous and, possibly, misleading. Sociological research is undertaken to describe or explain social phenomena. Research methodology refers to the system of rules and procedures that is followed in scientific investigation.

The common model for research involves a series of steps. First, the problem or topic to be researched is precisely stated, a crucial step; following this the researcher reviews the literature and the previous research relating to the problem. Thirdly, one or more hypotheses are formulated, being deduced from the theory relating to the problem. These are then restated as operational hypotheses, and the data required to test them are identified. The data-gathering procedure to be followed must be outlined in detail, and time-tabled step by step; the data are collected and analysed, and conclusions are drawn. The hypothesis may be supported, lending credence to the theory explaining the relationship between the variables, or the hypothesis may be refuted. The results are reported so that they are available to, and can be verified by, other researchers.

Data can be collected in a number of ways. The entire population in which the researcher is interested may be surveyed or, more commonly, a sample of the population is used. Examining existing sources of data that may be reused and reanalysed is an alternative. Some topics can be researched most effectively by observation; the researcher may be an onlooker recording the activities of a group or become a participant observer (that is become a member of the group being observed). Also, experiments involving small groups can sometimes be used. Each of these methods has an appropriate application, and the advantages and disadvantages of each must be assessed in relation to the topic to be researched.

The results of sociologists' research are reported in articles in sociological journals and in journals in closely related fields, in books, and in papers read at conferences. Government reports and reports done by consultants also publish sociologists' research findings.

Research results are sometimes reported in newspapers and popular magazines when the results are considered to be of public interest. This kind of coverage can be extremely helpful in getting research results widely known and in heightening public awareness of social issues.

However, you should consider in reading these press reports why the newspaper is covering the research. On the negative side there is the risk that either intentionally, or through ignorance or because of space limitations, the reporter picks up only part of the results, misinterprets the findings or makes generalizations beyond those warranted by the scope of the research, and ignores the limitations noted by the researcher. Newspapers also tend to sensationalize research findings to stimulate reader interest and sell more copies.

Newspaper reports of research results should be carefully analysed with these considerations in mind.

The mass media are the main source of information on current issues for the public. The reporting of research findings on social issues can influence public opinion and action. For example the reports of voters' preferences affect elections, influencing both voters' choices and politicians' campaigns. Views on censorship may be coloured by research into the impact of pornography. Research reports on such serious social problems as wife battering can heighten public awareness and lead to demands for stronger laws and increased funding to help women in abusive relationships. The second article in this section on sex education is an example of reporting that stimulates people's opinions on family-life education in schools.

The first article in this section, on the Canadian census, deals with the problems of non-response in data collection.

Some Difficulties With Data Gathering

INTRODUCTION

In Canada a major census is taken every ten years, in 1971, 1981, 1991, and 2001 with a less detailed census every five years. The results are widely used by researchers in many different disciplines, by business, and by government planners.

In the planning prior to taking the census, as in the planning of any research, there are many practical problems. Appropriate steps must be taken to resolve these or the research results may be seriously biased. The difficulties discussed in this article relate to the response rate to the census questionnaire.

This article relates to preparations for the 1981 Census. The same problems as well as new ones will arise with the next census in cities, towns and rural areas across Canada. Imagine yourself in the position of planning the enumeration of the population of Vancouver, or another Canadian city or town. Think about the difficulties involved. Consider carefully all the ways in which the response rate can be increased.

Census counting on undercounted

By Gillian Shaw

As the June 3 census date approaches, Statistics Canada has targeted Vancouver with measures to remedy the worst counting job in the country.

"B.C. is the worst province," census information officer Chris Mousseau said.

"In the 1971 census we missed three per cent of the population – that means we only counted 97 per cent... we have the highest undercount of all the provinces."

Mousseau said the problem is a language one. "We realize that in B.C. one of the largest areas of undercount is with the people who may not understand or speak English."

Supply and Services Minister, Jean Jacques Blais, who is responsible for Statistics Canada, said in Vancouver recently that enumeration is made more difficult by the fact many immigrants, legal and otherwise, are anxious about giving information to government officials.

Speaking to the Vancouver Board of Trade, Blais said: "British Columbia has many legal immigrants who have made enormous sacrifices to come to this country... tragically, some of our immigrants are illegals and live in constant fear of being found out by government officials."

"There is no reason for anyone to fear the census. In fact, there are many reasons why they should cooperate with the enumerators. Why, they should make sure that they are included in the national head count."

Blais repeated the often used assurance there is a law guaranteeing the confidentiality of census information.

"The act absolutely prohibits the disclosure of any information that would allow an individual person or household to be identified," he said.

Statistics Canada has introduced eight new programs designed to help overcome the undercount problem.

● Languages of different neighborhoods will be spoken by census staff, as much as possible.

● Store-front operations will be opened in cooperation with community groups.

● Pamphlets will be published in Chinese, Punjabi, Italian, Spanish and Portuguese; flyers will be published in 20 languages; posters will be distributed in 13 languages.

Concepts to consider:

Bias, mass media, non-response, population, response rate, sample.

● A telephone assistance program will be run from May 28 to June 5, with service in several languages. The number, listed on a flyer printed in 21 languages, will be handed out with the questionnaire to households where English is not understood.

● Education information packages have been distributed to all B.C. and Yukon schools and to teachers of English as a second language.

● Special programming on ethnic radio and television will focus on the census. Radio station CJVB is translating interviews on census topics into several languages.

● A slide show, to be used by liaison officers in speaking to various ethnic groups has been translated into Chinese, Punjabi and Italian.

● A multilingual census display will tour shopping centres in the Vancouver area starting May 15 and run for three weeks.

Statistics Canada has hired an ethnic officer, Angela Kan, to coordinate the ethnic census effort, Mousseau said.

Mousseau said the high migration rate to B.C. also plays havoc with the census. The current rental situation is another factor contributing to the discrepancy between the number of people enumerated and the number of people actually living in B.C. The large number of illegal suites means some households do not even receive a census form.

Mousseau said the housing shortage means census officers have to exercise a little ingenuity in finding people.

"Many people may not be living in what we call regular housing," he said. "We might have to go into Stanley Park and count the people sleeping there."

Age is a factor, Mousseau said.

"B.C. has a large number of people in the 19 to 24 age range. This has traditionally been an area of undercount," he said.

Almost 4,000 people in British Columbia have been hired to carry out the census. The census, taken every five years, will cost $11.50 per household over four years.

In Vancouver, a census form will be dropped off at every household starting May 25. People are asked to fill out the form on June 3 and mail it back to Statistics Canada.

People living in small towns and rural areas will have the form picked up after June 3 by the person who delivered it.

A basic 12-question form will be delivered to every household. One in five households will get an additional 32 questions to answer on such subjects as income, occupation, religion, and household payments.

The Sun, Vancouver, Tuesday, May 19, 1981, p. A11.

QUESTIONS

1. Does the Canadian census take a sample of the population, or the whole population, or both? What advantages does each of these methods have? What disadvantages does each have?

2. Non-response is a problem in any survey. Who is most likely to be missed by the census enumerators? Why? List both those mentioned in the article and other groups that are likely to be missed.

3. Are these groups likely to be significantly different from the rest of the population? Will this bias the results? Explain carefully.

4. Summarize the steps that the census planners have taken to ensure that non-response will be kept to a minimum. Do you think these will solve the problem?

5. In what ways can the mass media assist, or hinder, the census planners?

6. The census is conducted in early June. Why? What difficulties can you see to conducting it at other times of the year?

7. What further points can you make regarding difficulties and their solution, in undertaking a large survey such as the census?

8. As a result of what you have learned about the methods of taking the census, would you consider its results a reliable data source? Explain your opinion.

9. Should people be legally required to complete the census form as is currently the case?

Assessing the Credibility of Newspaper Reports of Surveys

INTRODUCTION

Newspapers report the results of research done by individuals and organizations when the topic of the research is of general public interest. Sex education in schools definitely falls into this category.

Knowing the basic principles of research methodology is helpful in assessing reports on survey research that appear in the press. Some research is reported in a manner that is balanced and accurate. However, catering to readers' interest may lead reporters to single out parts of the research for special emphasis, ignore the rest, or draw conclusions that are unwarranted given the scope of the research. Space restrictions often preclude detailed reporting.

Would you accept as reliable the information contained in the following report?

Sex education favored by 83% in survey

OTTAWA (CP)—Eighty-three per cent of Canadians believe sex education should be taught in schools, but only 50 per cent of the country's schools offer such courses, suggest two surveys released today by the Planned Parenthood Federation of Canada.

The surveys also indicate that most people, when they were children, received little information about sex from their parents, but would have liked to have been told more.

Although half of Canada's schools now provide sex education, most rural schools have no such courses and teachers often have little or no special training in the area.

"These surveys show a clear gap between what Canadians want and what the educational system is giving them," Dr. David Moores, federation president, said.

In one survey, conducted by Gallup for the federation, 1,063 adults were asked their views on sex education.

Eighty-three per cent of the respondents said sex education should be taught in schools. Fourteen per cent were opposed and three per cent were undecided.

Older people and those with little education, low incomes and no children at home tended to be more opposed to sex education in the schools.

Ninety-four per cent of respondents said parents should discuss sex with their children. Five per cent were opposed and one per cent was unsure.

Older people and those whose first language is neither French nor English were most opposed to parent-child talks on sex. Only about 20 per cent of the respondents said their parents discussed the "facts of life" with them before they reached age 12. About 75 per cent did not have these discussions and the remainder did not respond or could not remember.

Sixty-four per cent said they would have liked more information on sex while growing up. Twenty-nine per cent said they had no such wish and seven per cent were undecided.

French-speaking respondents, women and those with children at home were more likely to say they wished they had received more sex education as a child.

Almost 90 per cent of respondents said everyone should have the right to use birth control, seven per cent were opposed and the remainder unsure.

Fifty-nine per cent said they have used birth control, 39 per cent said they have not and two per cent would not say.

Prior use of birth control was highest among people aged 30 to 50, women and those whose first language is French or English.

British Columbia, where 76 per cent of respondents said they have used birth control, had the highest

Concepts to consider:

Bias, correlation, explanation, questionnaire, reliability, sample, sample size, survey, validity.

QUESTIONS

1. Define sample. Explain the different types of samples briefly.

2. The first paragraph of this record contains statements relating to the number of Canadians who believe sex education should be taught in schools, and the number of schools who offer such courses. Do you accept these statements after considering the type and size of the sample? Discuss.

3. Explain what is meant by correlation.

4. There are several statements in this report that imply a correlation—cite two of them. What is the connection, if any, between a correlation, a cause, and an explanation?

5. What are the important criteria to keep in mind when writing questions for questionnaires?

6. Write five questions that could have been used to get the percentages cited for the first survey in this newspaper report.

7. Is the subject matter of the second questionnaire liable to bias the results? What steps can be taken to guard against bias?

8. Does the response rate to the second questionnaire invalidate the results?

9. Is this newspaper report sensationalizing the survey results? Explain your answer and give examples.

10. Would you accept the information conveyed in this report as reliable? Why or why not?

---

rate of usage.

In the second survey, questionnaires were sent to officials representing 625 school districts in the country and responses were received from 356.

Among the respondents, 50 per cent said they offered a "family life education" program and 33 per cent said they were optimistic they would implement a program within a few years.

Eighty-seven per cent of urban schools had a program, compared with 52 per cent of schools serving a mix of rural, town and city pupils and only 25 per cent of rural schools.

Winnipeg Free Press, Thursday, September 27, 1984, p. 1.

FIND A CLIPPING

Find a short article in a newspaper or magazine discussing an issue that could be a subject for research.

Define the topic for research precisely. Your topic need not include everything in the article.

What methods of data collection would you use for investigating this topic? For example, would you use a survey method; observation or participant observation; an experiment; existing sources of data; or a combination of some of these. Explain the advantages and limitations of the method, or combination of methods, you advocate.

3

Culture

The sociological meaning of the term culture is broader than the everyday use of the word. In sociology, the term refers to the totality of what is learned by individuals as members of a society. It embraces all the ideas, knowledge, traditions, behaviour, beliefs, and values that are widely held by individuals in that society.

Culture is learned from, and shared with, others. Language, gestures, beliefs, values and norms are widely understood within the society. Because it is learned and reinforced through being shared with others, culture influences actions, and structures our perceptions of the world. Language is key in perpetuating, sharing and passing on to succeeding generations our perceptions of the world and ways of relating to other people. Culture makes it possible for us to live with others, and thus makes society itself possible.

The knowledge and understanding that is shared involves both non-material beliefs, values and norms, and the purpose and meaning of material items. Knowledge accumulates and is passed on between people and to each succeeding generation. The concept of material culture encompasses the things we have and use. Much of the knowledge we share relates to the function and symbolic meaning of artifacts, such as chairs, tables, baseball bats, art works, records, cars, clothing, computers, pencils, and so on. These take on significance only when we understand what they are used for, and how we should understand the symbolic meanings they encapsulate. Clothing, for example, keeps us warm and covered, but also conveys messages to others about the kind of person we are, the social class to which we belong, and how much we choose to conform.

Beliefs, values and norms are part of the non-material culture. Beliefs are convictions about the way things are, and are shared with others: religious beliefs are an example, as are political beliefs. Values are socially shared views on what is right and wrong, what is good and what is deplorable. Values can relate to both the goals worth striving for and to acceptable means of achieving these goals. Ideology refers to a set of beliefs and values held by a group or by members of society that justifies the particular interests of the group and repudiates alternative ideas that would undermine the group's position. Dominant ideologies, those that are the most prevalent in the society, uphold the status quo.

Norms are rules of behaviour; the rules that are strictly adhered to by the majority of people are the laws. Formal sanctions are applied to those who violate the law. Mores are norms that incur severe social disapproval. If they are violated, sanctions can be very severe. Folkways describe the way people usually behave in given circumstances. The social sanctions for violating folkways are less severe and may even be absent. We know roughly how we are expected to act in most situations. Usually the norms are known, understood and taken for granted, and so most people do not stop to examine them. People use their own definition of the situation they are in, subconsciously apply the accepted social norms, and act accordingly.

Beliefs, values and norms are shared with others, and thus they constitute guidelines or a framework for living with others within the society. There is wide scope for individuals to decide what to think and how to act as individuals, but the cultural framework is always there as a constraint within which they must perform.

Within a complex society there are a variety of sub-cultures with distinctive beliefs, values, and norms. Many groups are concerned with maintaining their own language and distinctive way of life while also participating in the common culture of Canadian society. These sub-cultures may flourish, but only if their members are concerned and committed to using their own language and protecting their sub-culture from erosion, actively working to keep it alive, and passing on the culture to the next generation.

Both material and non-material items from other cultures have been integrated into what has become "Canadian culture." The process of cultural diffusion refers to the way in which cultural items are adopted and adapted from other societies and become part of Canadian culture.

As each society maintains its own distinct culture which frames how people within that society think of themselves and others, it follows that cross-cultural misunderstandings can arise when people travel. If people are unreflective as to how different perceptions can arise or are convinced of the superiority of their own culture, they are likely to experience difficulties and misunderstand much while travelling or working in different societies. Such people are termed ethnocentric. Ethnocentrism can produce much misunderstanding and antagonism, an issue with which the first article in this section deals. The opposite view, cultural relativism, recognizes that something as simple as a handshake, or as complex as religious belief, may have a particular relevance in its own cultural context and should be understood and appreciated as having a special meaning.

The second article deals with opinions on changing a fundamental system in our culture, that of how we measure. All our systems of measurement have come from other cultures, and have been copied and adapted to the needs of Canadian culture. The controversy over using a metric system of measurement has aroused continuing hostility in many people.

The third article describes research into the popularity of yard sales and examines the social interaction that surrounds buying and selling.

Cultural Relativity

INTRODUCTION

Business today is multinational. Consequently, many business people travel to other countries to propose and seal contracts. Business deals involve the trust that both parties will honour the spirit of the contract as well as the legal aspects, but trust presumes mutual understanding and agreement. Unless a conscious effort is made to break out of our own cultural mould, our understanding of others and their situations will be based only on what is learned within our own cultural setting. We need to become aware that ways of doing things that seem "right" and "natural" to us are in fact relative to our culture. To others, their way of doing things is right and natural and ours is strange.

This article discusses some of the cultural differences that can get in the way of creating successful business relationships.

Cultural awareness can make wheeling and dealing easier

By Ben Fiber

Canadian executives negotiating in foreign countries without doing some homework on local customs run the risk of jeopardizing deals and souring business relationships.

Correct observance of the different cultural taboos and practices throughout the world can be crucial, winning considerable good will before negotiations. Ignorance of them can create psychological barriers.

But many business travellers often are unaware of the finer points of custom in the countries in which they plan to deal.

Religion, politics and social niceties, for instance, play a far greater role in the cultures of Japan, China and the Middle East than they do in Canada.

Finding out how to behave is not necessarily difficult, as sources are plentiful. The Canadian Chamber of Commerce and counterpart bodies abroad, embassies and consulates, and federal trade officials can provide valuable insights into the foreign ways of doing business.

Foreign business people may take entirely different approaches to a deal than those expected by the unwary Canadian.

For example, the Canadian may find he has to work hard for months before securing a contract he wants in Japan. The Japanese regard any business arrangement as a symbiotic relationship between two corporations, as well as a means to profit.

Also, the traditional North American habit of self-introduction on first meeting is discouraged. The Japanese prefer to make initial contact through a mutual business acquaintance or government official.

Negotiations tend to be marked by much more formality than in Canada. Greater emphasis is placed on clothing, form of address and the exchange of business cards.

The culmination of discussions may leave the Canadian businessperson dissatisfied. The Japanese require lots of time to work over the small print and rarely will produce a detailed contract on the spot. Instead, letters often will be exchanged confirming that agreement has been reached.

In the Middle East, protocol can be just as important in negotiating a deal.

Arabs feel they should be well acquainted with the people involved in transactions, and several visits may be required before an agreement is reached.

Customs outside the boardroom also may have an impact on the course of negotiations. For example, little business is conducted during the Moslem holy month of Ramadan.

Arabs place great emphasis on handshaking. Most travel guides to the Middle East stress that the visitor's hand may be held for some time while in conversation.

When seated, open display of the sole of the shoe indicates disrespect, as would proffering food or drink in the left hand.

Travellers should also take note of the strict Moslem countries where alcohol is banned, such as Saudi Arabia. However, some countries, such as Egypt, have adopted a more relaxed attitude.

Above all, patience is the keynote. While Arabs insist on punctuality, visitors may be kept waiting while their hosts deal with more pressing business. In their order of priorities, the foreigner is at the bottom.

Negotiations also can be a frustrating experience in China. The Chinese may take frequent breaks – sometimes for days – while they develop their negotiating positions.

The Chinese place great emphasis on developing friendships along with business links. Canadians may find the Chinese making lengthy overtures to know and understand them.

The Chinese demand detailed knowledge of the technical aspects of an operation. Business people who intend to make long yardage should have the expertise themselves or bring along the personnel who do. This means the Canadian company is serious about doing business in China, said one guide to doing business with the Chinese.

There is no greater contrast to the business practices of Japan and China than in West Germany, where business people prefer to get down to hard bargaining quickly. But West Germans, who are more formal than most other Europeans when doing business, make up in hospitality later for what appears to be an initial lack of warmth.

Wherever they are going, travellers are well advised to find out when the major vacation season occurs and what the public holidays are.

The summer holiday period can be a difficult time to conduct business. In Paris, for example, many hotels and restaurants are closed in late July and August and few businesses operate at full strength.

Then there are special holidays such as the Mardi Gras season in Brazil when business all but grinds to a halt at the end of February.

Dealings in Eastern Europe carry their own brand of problems. In each country, western business people face different regulations, including restrictions on travel and trade, as well as poor service.

Business people will require enormous patience in dealing with the red tape they will come up against.

The Globe and Mail, Toronto, Saturday, February 27, 1982, p. B26.

Concepts to consider:

Culture, cultural relativism, ethnocentrism, norms, values.

QUESTIONS

1. How do sociologists use the term culture?

2. How does culture influence behaviour?

3. Define norm. From the article, identify two examples of norms that differ from Canadian norms.

4. What are social values? Differing values mean that what is considered desirable in a business deal may vary between cultures. Provide one example of this from the article.

5. Why does the writer of this article think it is important for Canadian business executives to do some homework on the culture of the country in which they will be negotiating? Explain carefully. Go beyond the article; do not merely quote from it.

6. In the fourth paragraph of the article Ben Fiber says, "Religion, politics and social niceties, for instance, play a far greater role in the cultures of Japan, China and the Middle East than they do in Canada." Do you think this is really true, or it is just that we know our own culture so well that we do not recognize the role of these factors? Explain your answer.

7. Define ethnocentrism. How is ethnocentrism illustrated in the article? Give an example of ethnocentrism from your own life experience.

8. How might Canadians have advantages in business or travel in foreign countries over people from other countries?

CAC viewpoint: On metric conversion

Cultural Diffusion and the Way We Measure

INTRODUCTION

Among the cultural conventions that we share as members of society are systems of measurement. Standard measures are important in international trade. In the exchange of goods between countries some standardization is necessary if the imported items are to be used in conjunction with those produced elsewhere.

Ways of measuring are also significant at a personal level. Commonly used measurements acquire an intuitive and symbolic meaning in people's minds. Altering the system of measurement arouses hostility because many people feel confused by the new system; the switch to metric is an example of this. The new metric measures lack the intuitive meaning attached to the old system and make people feel insecure. Older people may also feel that their past learning and accumulated experience is negated.

Changing an important item of culture is always difficult, and the change may take a while to be accepted. The editorial from Canadian Consumer explains the views of the Consumer Association of Canada on the process of metric conversion.

By Barbara Shand, President, Consumers Association of Canada

As early as 1962, and well before the federal government's commitment to metric conversion, CAC publicly urged the adoption of the metric system in Canada. If properly implemented, we argued, the metric system held great promise for Canadian consumers in the domestic market place, and for Canadian industry in international markets.

Since the passage of the Consumer Packaging and Labelling Act of 1970, CAC has been represented on several committees involved in Canada's conversion to metric. Our participation has left us, particularly since the mid-1970s, with a growing sense of frustration and disillusionment – *not* with the goal of metric conversion, but with the manner in which government and segments of industry have gone about implementing it.

The promise of metric

CAC is often asked why we have so consistently supported the goal of metric conversion. In part, we simply recognized the worldwide trend to the metric system, a trend which seemed to make inevitable Canada's adoption of the metric measurement. More than 95 per cent of the world's population today reside in countries using the metric system. Only four coun-

tries (Brunei, Burma, and the two Yemens) have not yet announced an intention to switch to metric.

This trend has critical implications for a country involved in international trade like Canada. Australia, which has disbanded its metric conversion board following total conversion to metric, accepts imported goods in metric sizes only, except in a few specialized cases. Japan prohibits the use of non-metric units for commercial transactions and documentation, except in a few traditional craft industries. By December 31, 1989, the member countries of the European Economic Community must be using standard metric units for trade purposes.

Canadian critics of the metric system are fond of suggesting that our largest trading partner, the United States, has "given up" on metric. In fact, the U.S. *Metric Converstion Act,* Adopted in 1975, is still in force. It is true that the U.S. Metric Board was dissolved in October 1982, but its functions were transferred to the U.S. Commerce Department's Office of Metric Programs.

As important as these international considerations are, CAC called for metric measurement primarily because of its potential advantages to consumers. The old imperial system of measurement may seem simple and straightforward to those of us who grew up with it. In fact, compared with the metric system, it is complex and cumbersome. Learning the imperial system means memorizing such information as 1 mile equals 5280 feet, 1 pound equals 16 ounces, and that water freezes at 32°F and boils at 212°F. Learning to use the metric system is primarily a matter of learning where to place the decimal point — 1 kilometre (km) equals 1000 metres (m), 1 millilitre (mL) equals .001 litres (L), and water freezes at 0°C and boils at 100°C.

Related to its relative simplicity is the fact that the metric system, unlike imperial measurement, is internationally standardized. While imperial measures often vary from one country to another (the difference between the American and Canadian gallon, for example), metric measures are the same everywhere. And while an ounce may be fluid, troy or avoirdupois, there is only one litre! Metric units have been standardized through international agreements dating to the Treaty of the Metre in 1875 and culminating in the adoption in 1960 of the International System of Units.

In CAC's view, the relative simplicity of metric measurement should create a simpler and more rational market place for consumers. The metric system should help to reverse the proliferation of package sizes confronting consumers and encourage both comparison shopping and unit pricing.

Disappointments

In supporting metric conversion, CAC assumed the new system would be implemented so these consumer advantages would be realised. We acknowledge that there have been successes in conversion. Many industries, meeting under the umbrella of the Metric Commission, have adopted guidelines calling for "hard conversion" (the adoption of manageable and rational package sizes such as 500 grams (g)).

In recent years, however, CAC has encountered disappointment after disappointment in the conversion process. Some industries have opted for "soft conversion", leaving consumers with "funny numbers", such as 454 g and 298 mL. Others have chosen a combination of hard and soft conversion.

The result of all of this has been an increase in consumer confusion, precisely what CAC hoped metric conversion would eliminate.

CAC has not, as some have suggested, done a sudden "about-face" on the issue of metric conversion. We remain as convinced as ever that *if properly implemented*, metric conversion will create long-term benefits for Canadian consumers. In various public statements and articles, including the April 1982 "Viewpoint", we have pointed to the shortcomings of the current implementation process. In late 1983, our frustration reached a point where we felt compelled to inform the federal government that we are re-evaluating our participation in the conversion process.

Don't turn back

The federal Department of Consumer and Corporate Affairs has failed to insist on rational conversion, and the result has left consumers with the worst of all worlds—an imperial system measured in metric units.

Canadian consumers are angry over the chaos and confusion they are finding in the market place. They have every right to be; metric conversion has not yet lived up to its promise. The answer, however, is not to turn back. International trade is increasingly conducted in metric measurements. Maintaining two systems of measurement – one for domestic use and one for international trade – would be inefficient and expensive.

Canadian government and industry promised consumers that they would benefit from metric conversion. It is high time they honoured that promise. They must press on to make the implementation process as quick and painless as possible.

Canadian Consumer, May 1984, p. 49.

Concepts to consider:

Cultural diffusion, education, government, social change, socialization, symbol.

QUESTIONS

1. Define cultural diffusion. Give three examples of items that did not originate in Canada that are now part of Canadian culture. Cite three that are Canadian creations.

2. Is the metric system of measurement an example of cultural diffusion?

3. If peoples of the world do not all speak the same language, wear the same dress, believe in the same religion, why is it necessary to adopt the same measurement system? Or is it?

4. Why should Canadians "go metric" according to CAS?

5. Can government change culture? Discuss and give examples from the article.

6. How many times today have you bought, used or accepted something in a measured amount? List the items.

7. Can you measure some things with reasonable accuracy without using a mesuring tool like a ruler, measuring cup, scale or thermometer? How do you manage to do this? Explain precisely.

8. "On the domestic scene many consumers resist the introduction of metric." Why do people resist changes in the method of measurement? Give and explain all the reasons you can think of.

9. Would you consider a system of measurement to be a part of culture? Explain why.

The Norms of Buying and Selling

INTRODUCTION

In every culture, goods and services are exchanged in specific, routinized, well understood ways which have evolved in that culture's economy over time. Individuals with goods or services to offer, offer them for sale or exchange. Those that need the goods or services acquire them after negotiation or acceptance of the terms of the sale or barter.

The items offered for sale, whether physically tangible goods or intangible services, have values both to the buyer and seller: their usefulness or value to the buyer must be greater than to the seller if a bargain is to be struck or a sale made. The knowledge of the worth, value and/or usefulness is learned from living in the society, and of course the buyers' personal likes or dislikes influence their choices.

Goods can be bought in a variety of different places, and the norms that guide our behaviour as buyers vary according to the place. Have you ever stopped to consider how you act when you are shopping at a supermarket, at a farmers' market, or at a yard sale?

Researchers find yard sales a 'way of life'

KINGSTON, Ont. (CP)—What makes people leave the comfort of their homes to spend weekends hunting for bargains that neighbors and strangers have dragged out of attics, basements, garages and closets?

Most don't stop to wonder why they've joined the millions of North American yard sale aficionados over the past two decades. They're too busy pawing through stuff and plotting their next stop.

But Queen's University sociologists Mary and James Maxwell have discovered that yard sales and flea markets have become a way of life.

Social phenomenon

They're a social phenomenon, a return to old values, a chance in these days of impersonal, immense chain owned stores to exchange pleasantries and use the bric-a-brac of previous generations to reminisce about "the good old days," the two researchers say.

Older people especially seem to benefit from yard sales and flea markets, the Maxwells say. In a less-commercial, more personalized setting, it's a way to combat the growing alienation of society.

"Friends told us that the elderly participate more in yard sales," James Maxwell said in an interview, "It's not that they buy, it's that they're not as welcome in commercial establishments if they're not shopping."

"They can socialize, learn and share," Mary Maxwell adds. "That's not something you can do in a supermarket."

For some people, however, yard sales and flea markets are a way to make money, either selling or buying marketable bargains. Guide books for successful sales have even been published.

Yard sales limited

But pressured by merchants who fear a loss of business, some municipalities—such as nearby Trenton—have passed regulations to limit the number of yard sales a family can hold in a year.

Concepts to consider:

Alienation, data collection, market system, material culture, non-material culture, norms, social class, social interaction, symbol.

The Maxwells spent eight years on their study, interviewing participants in Ontario and Quebec on both sides of the tables. Although James Maxwell says "my affair with garage sales is almost over, except if they're next door," the couple say that after putting away their notebooks they'll miss meeting people – and wandering away with just the right thing for their den or kitchen.

"For some people it's enormously reassuring that the market system works," James Maxwell says.

"The category of collectables and the social acceptance of the collector's role has facilitated the growth of the market," the study says. "In particular, the redefinition of collecting as a middle- and even lower-middle-class pastime, and not simply the perserve of the wealthy, has created a mass market of redistribution."

Winnipeg Free Press, Thursday, September 20, 1984 p. 38.

QUESTIONS

1. Define culture. What is meant by material culture? How do the items of the material culture acquire meaning or usefulness?

2. Explain what is meant by the market system, and why it can be considered part of the culture.

3. Outline the norms you follow when you buy in a supermarket or large department store.

4. What is different about the buyer's behaviour when buying at a yard sale compared with a supermarket? Use the article and your imagination.

5. What is meant by alienation? Why is buying goods at a yard sale less alienating for some shoppers than buying things at a supermarket?

6. The last paragraph makes reference to "the social acceptance of the collector's role." Do you need "social acceptance" before you collect things? Explain and give an example.

7. Explain what you understand by social class. What role could collecting certain types of items have in designating social class?

8. What method of data collection would you think these two Queen's University sociologists used in their research into yard sales and flea markets?

FIND A CLIPPING

Find a clipping that describes a group of people getting extremely concerned or agitated over a social issue, and taking action in regard to it.

Read the article and explain the views of the group and what motivates them to action. Use the article (and your own knowledge if you know more about the group).

Explain what is meant by ideology. Do the opinions, views or political stance taken by the group you are discussing reflect an ideology? Explain as fully as you can the ideology and how it underlies the group's actions.

4

The Mass Media

Communication is crucial in any society. It is by communicating that culture is created and sustained. Ideas, knowledge, ways of doing things, ways of behaving, beliefs, values, and attitudes are disseminated by the media throughout society. Information about new ideas, new inventions, new forms of music and entertainment thus become part of public awareness. Indeed, partly as a result of the media, our culture has a great deal in common with the culture of the other industrialized countries of the world. Designed to communicate to large audiences, the mass media have created a mass culture.

Mass media refers to all ways of communicating with large audiences—television, radio, newspapers, magazines, comics, records, tapes, movies, pocketbooks. The mass media play an important role in our society in transmitting news and information, and in entertaining. Some of the mass media reach and influence us every day. Imagine a day without radio, T.V., newspapers, tapes, or books!

The fairness and impartiality of the news and information spread by the media is often hotly debated. The sources of possible bias are many. In any news account, a reporter, an editor or producer must make a selection of facts and a judgment on what is, or is not, important. This selection of information, facts, or opinions, and the perceptions of the individuals involved, can result in distortion or bias even when the intention is to be impartial.

The dominant ideology influences the thinking of those who decide the content of the reports and views expressed in the media and is thereby reinforced in the minds of the audience. Our beliefs in free enterprise, capitalism, democracy, and romantic love would be examples of these. Countervailing ideologies, like communism or socialism, may also be covered, but often with negative comment and the use of pejoratives: "radical," "perversion," for example. Watch for the use of "loaded words" and adjectives that flag favoured and disfavoured opinions.

Entertainment items on T.V., radio, in magazines, and pocketbooks convey values and norms of behaviour to viewers or readers. Television in particular is a powerful image-maker and conveys to viewers, in a very subtle way, a host of beliefs, values and norms that may be absorbed sub-consciously and become part of the "world view" of the audiences.

All forms of media are subject to financial pressure and influence. To survive, much of the media must get advertising revenue. They must tailor their writing or programming to attract readers, viewers or listeners so that they can sustain or increase the size of their audience, to attract advertisers.

Grants from the federal and provincial governments are also a source of funding for the CBC, the ethnic press, radio, and T.V. Trusts, or large corporations and churches, may also contribute grants. Grants may by given with no strings attached, but funding bodies may wish to exert influence over the recipients of their largess. Small organizations, interest groups and ethnic groups who wish to have their own newspaper, or programming on T.V. or radio, are particularly vulnerable to outside pressure since their operations are often uneconomic with only a small audience to provide support.

Pressure can be applied to all forms of media by particular interest groups with a strong desire to get their views across to the public. Pressure may be applied to politicians to regulate the print or electronic media, possibly by imposing some form of censorship to ban whatever is deemed undesirable. The C.R.T.C. (Canadian Radio and Television Commission), the federal regulatory body, attempts to ensure equal coverage in time of both sides of controversial issues. This agency regulates standards in broadcasting as well as the number of stations in communities. The provincial Film Boards rate movies, and the various press councils mediate problems and seek to maintain freedom of the press.

The first article which follows deals with the role of the media in shaping ideas and giving information. The second article deals with issues that relate to the financing of newspapers. The third article examines the links between T.V. programming, advertising and the audience.

The Media's Role in Political Campaigns

INTRODUCTION

The leaders of the federal political parties referred to in this particular article are John Turner, Brian Mulroney, and Edward Broadbent, but the arguments apply equally well to any leader and any political campaign.

The article draws attention to the structure of the media, particularly T.V. and newspapers, and of political parties, and the process by which political campaign managers can manipulate the media to attain their party goals. The media have been, it is argued, subverted from serving the public and voters to serving the political parties.

Consider the extent to which this is true and whether what this writer suggests would reverse this trend and lead to the public being better informed on political affairs.

A special challenge for Canada's media

By Michael Nolan

(Michael Nolan, a professor of Journalism at the University of Western Ontario and former broadcaster, explains in the following article how the mass media are often captives of politicians and their media advisers at election time.)

"Television has come into its own, and political journalism has veered toward total irrelevance, during recent election campaigns." — The Royal Commission on Newspapers, July 1, 1981.

With the Liberal and Conservative parties boasting ideal leaders for the electronic age of campaigning, the September federal election promises to be the ultimate mass-media exercise. The New Democratic Party, which in its early years stressed a pure party philosophy and shunned advertising techniques, has also shown a capacity to adjust to the demands of media politics.

Therefore, the media, in this election, face an onerous responsibility in attempting to provide a balanced and even-handed treatment of the leaders, candidates and issues.

In the federal campaigns of 1974, '79 and '80, journalists were none too successful, despite attempts to assess the leaders and policy positions of all parties. The Kent Commission noted that "the most effective campaign strategies were those that deliberately limited leaders to one or two media events each day where they addressed selected partisan audiences."

These staged appearances "almost completely supplanted authentic contact with voters and precluded any intelligent discussion of issues. Television was forced to report them daily, while print journalists were reduced to criticizing the television campaign. That did nothing to inform citizens of the substance of party differences on the major issues facing the country."

Now that Canadians are in the midst of their 33rd federal election, the question to be addressed is whether the media can serve any longer as an honest channel of communication between politicians and the people.

If journalists are to be the filters and voters' eyes and ears, they will have to reassess some of their recently established practices. To avoid being merely captives of the political leaders and their skilled advisers, the media might have to consider adjustments in their style of reporting.

First, campaign coverage that is less leader-oriented probably would allow for a more meaningful discussion of regional candidates and issues. Second, the media might also play more to their strengths, with T.V. focusing on breaking or "spot" news and newspapers providing almost exclusively the interpretation, commentary and independent analysis.

In this way, the broadcasting and print media would be reinforcing their respective efforts rather than adhering to schedules or party leaders and their daily ration of visuals for the nightly T.V. news.

Since its inception some 30 years ago, T.V. has placed new demands on politicians and advertising agencies have moved front and centre on the campaign stage. During elections, the media have had to try to circumvent these strategists who have become adept at assisting politicians to control their campaign environment.

For example, before Pierre Trudeau's first campaign as Liberal leader in 1968, MacLaren Advertising advised the party to avoid the sizeable purchase of conventional "spot" announcements on T.V. George Elliott, the agency's representative on the Liberal campaign committee, viewed the 1968 campaign as a contest between the T.V. networks rather than the parties.

The CTV network had won favorable reviews for its coverage of the Conservative party's 1967 leadership convention. The CBC similarly had benefited from its reporting on the 1968 Liberal convention where Mr. Trudeau had been chosen. In Mr. Elliott's view, the election campaign would be a "rubber match" between the networks.

This journalistic approach would give all the political lead-

ers, but especially Mr. Trudeau, greater news coverage than ever. Mr. Elliott argued that Mr. Trudeau could hold his own in any television encounter and that "the media were tame, tame pussy cats" in 1968.

During the four elections since the memorable campaign of Trudeaumania, a growing emphasis has been placed on the projection of party leaders by campaign strategists. In the process, the media have often succumbed to manipulation by professionals skilled in the tactics of mass persuasion who recognized that journalists facing regular filing deadlines could be made to provide a kind of uniform coverage of leaders, depending on the structure of the campaign.

Thus pseudo-events have become the order of the day during elections and the pack-like behavior of journalists has shown them to be easy victims. They are, as Timothy Crouse explained in his informative book, *The Boys on the Bus*, "like a pack of hounds sicked on a fox."

While the media's attention has been focused on party leaders in recent campaigns, there has been, at the same time, less emphasis given to electoral attitudes in the various regions of the country.

In the words of the Kent Commission, "newspapers appear to have been heavily influenced by television coverage with its emphasis on attacks and counter-attacks, leadership, color, action and the horserace aspect of the campaigns. Local and regional issues have been neglected."

This centralized kind of coverage has meant that important political issues, such as the economy or energy, have received little meaningful debate in the media or, when they do, the discussion frequently flows from a central

Canada perspective. A shift from the preoccupation with party leaders to regional issues would provide more balanced coverage and enable the media to set their own campaign agenda without having to rely on the itineraries of John Turner, Brian Mulroney and Ed Broadbent.

Campaign '84 presents the media with a special challenge, since the old-line parties have new leaders whose images seem made for T.V. and whose policy positions appear similar. In a summertime election with fresh air, sunshine and shopping plaza crowds greeting Mr. Turner and Mr. Mulroney, it will be tempting for journalists to stress the personalized and image aspects of the campaign.

Yet while T.V. must capture the public response to all party leaders on the hustings, it rests with the print medium to analyze whatever policy and ideological differences exist or develop among them.

T.V., a highly impressionistic medium, has shown it can communicate visually most immediate campaign developments. But it has limitations as a vehicle for indepth analysis of issues.

Still, the weakness of T.V. is the strength of print journalists. Newspapers, instead of rivalling T.V., might try, in this election campaign, to regain the impact they had on the public's political thinking before the advent of T.V.

With the electronic media and newspapers providing a more decentralized coverage and playing complementary rather than competing roles, Campaign '84 could usher in a new age of political journalism from which all Canadians would benefit.

The Globe and Mail, Toronto, Monday, July 23, 1984, p. 7.

Concepts to consider:

Mass media, politics, role performance, symbolic interaction.

QUESTIONS

1. Before radio and television, how did people learn about political candidates, and party policies when an election was called?

2. What does Michael Nolan say is "The major question to be addressed"?

3. What does Nolan identify as the major problems in the media coverage of political campaigns?

4. What are the ideal qualities of a leader in the electronic age of campaigning? Are these attributes essential for effective role performance in office?

5. Why have newspapers tended to report on what is also covered by T.V. rather than doing in-depth analyses of the political campaign?

6. What are some of the techniques of mass persuasion?

7. T.V., radio, and newspapers each have a unique means of communicating with the public. List what you see as the major strengths of each medium.

8. Explain exactly how you think Canadians would benefit from Michael Nolan's proposal that T.V. and newspapers should play separate roles in political coverage. If you disagree with the proposal explain why.

9. Since T.V. and newspapers appear to provide superficial coverage of elections, how can Canadians get more analysis and depth to interpret campaign issues?

Containing the Indians

Financing a Small Newspaper

INTRODUCTION

Freedom of the press is an important principle, but it is questionable whether much of the press is completely free. Newspapers have to finance themselves as does any other business. Daily newspapers with large circulations get 20% of their revenue from circulation and 80% from advertising. For the tabloids the percentages are somewhat different: 32% of revenue comes from circulation, the rest from advertising revenue.

Small circulation newspapers have a financial problem that is illustrated by this article on two newspapers written for the native people in Alberta. The revenue sources have to include grants from government or from elsewhere to help meet the costs of production (newsprint and printing), distribution, administrative, editorial and labour costs. The risk involved in accepting grants is that the newspaper may fall under the control of the revenue source. There is a possible conflict between allowing free expression of opinion and coverage of topics of concern to the minority groups and the interests of the grant giver.

By Frank Dabbs and Link Byfield

Alberta Indians were treated to a sharp lesson in humility last month by provincial Minister of Native Affairs Milton George Pahl (Edmonton Mill Woods). His normally quiet Native Secretariat became prominent three weeks ago for the revelation that it was dictating to the province's two major Indian newspapers what they should print if they want to sustain the provincial government grants upon which they depend. Last week, while the editors charged at a press conference that the government was undermining a decade of credibility-building on their part, Mr. Pahl replied calmly that "where there's public funding going in, don't expect me to be indifferent to what's coming out."

In Mr. Pahl's view, subscribers to the two "non-commercial newspapers" are not being told about what their provincial government is doing for them. His department is therefore insisting that the editors of southern Alberta's Kainai News (circulation 3,450) and northern Alberta's The AMMSA (circulation 6,500) budget some 15 per cent of their news space to coverage of provincial services and subjects. For either paper this would mean 104 pages of news copy per year: 46 on native and service organizations, 36 on the role of other government departments, 10 on Indian personality profiles, and 12 on current Indian issues. The details, as Indian Affairs envisions it, are to be worked out between government and editorial committees.

All this is particularly galling to the province's 50 or so Indian journalists, most of whom are part-time or freelance writers long accustomed to the reactions of suspicious Indian readers, band politicians and thin-skinned government officials. Canadian Indian journalism was born in Alberta when Edmonton broadcasters Eugene Steinhauer and Les Healy began a native-affairs radio program in 1967 for Edmonton's CKUA radio station. That led in 1969 to the Alberta Native Communications Society, a participant in the early-1970s Project Ironstar, a satellite television experiment sponsored by the federal government. At about the same time both weekly newspapers began as well. The southern Kainai News has continued without interruption. Edmonton's Native People, however, lost control of its budget and folded in disgrace in late 1982. It was replaced last year with The AMMSA (short for Aboriginal Multi-Media Society of Alberta). Between them, they reach virtually all Indians and Metis in the province. They also set the pattern for the 13 other Indian media societies that have followed them in all parts of Canada except New Brunswick.

The most frustrating feature of the business, according to Roy Pipenburg, communications officer of the Indian Association of Alberta, is that the papers can't sustain themselves through circulation and advertising revenues. This, he says, is hardly surprising given the economic dependency upon governments of the readership.

Such dependency became a humiliation for the two papers when, last winter, they began negotiating this year's provincial grant with Ronald Harrison, assistant general manager of the Alberta native secretariat. Kainai gets some $212,000 annually from the provincial government, and AMMSA about $132,000. (By contrast, the feds provide $276,000 and $434,000 respectively, and make no editorial stipulations.) Mr. Harrison made it plain, according to the editors, that the demand would stick, and both papers, unwilling to consent, entered the year with no assurance of provincial funding. Currently the papers are counter-offering to run a negotiable proportion of government-written material on pages clearly designated as having been bought.

The tougher stand has been taken by the Kainai paper's Indian News Media Society. "We are entitled to these grants without strings attached," declared Kainai editor Jacqueline A. Red Crow last week. The society's lawyer believes the government's demand appears to contradict its own stated policy of supporting "self-reliant development" of native newspapers allowing "independent expression of editorial opinion."

Mr. Pahl, an ex-boxer, isn't running away yet, however. "I'm not out to make this thing disagreeable," he explained last week, "but natives outside the political mainstream just aren't hearing about government programs." His department is now considering the Indians' counter-offer.

Alberta Report, May 7, 1984, p. 9.

Concepts to consider:

Censorship, ideology, influence, majority group, minority group, politics, power, social stratification, sub-culture, values.

QUESTIONS

1. Identify a number of the possible ways of communicating with all the native people in Alberta.

2. Why do the Indian people need newspapers specifically designed for them?

3. How do daily newspapers finance their production and distribution? Why can the Indian press not rely on these methods?

4. Suppose the Kainai News and The AMMSA could gain sufficient revenue from advertising to finance their production and distribution. Would they be free to print what they liked?

5. Is the government action described in the article equivalent to censorship? If you think it is not, could it develop into government censorship?

6. There is an apparent inconsistency in government policy in that the government on one hand tries to help the Indians and on the other hand tries to control them. What could be the cause of this contradiction?

7. What problems do you see in the editors' counter-offer of running government written material on pages designated as having been bought by the Provincial Government? Is this a solution?

8. Can you suggest other solutions?

9. Who has the power in this situation?

10. Would conflict theory provide an appropriate framework for analysing the relationship between the newspapers, their readers, and the government? Explain why or why not.

Connections Between Programmes, Audiences and Advertisers

INTRODUCTION

Advertising is a key source of income for many T.V. companies. The "product" the company can sell is access to the viewers of a particular programme. The amount companies can charge for an advertising slot depends on a variety of factors, including the size of the audience and the sex, age, and social class composition of the viewers (as determined by audience ratings).

Advertisers look for a return on their advertising dollar in the form of higher sales, and will, therefore, pick advertising spots in programmes that offer access to potential buyers of their particular products. Besides the characteristics of the audience, the content of a particular programme will influence companies' choice of whether or not to advertise. Many companies do not want their products associated with certain types of programming. The supply of advertising slots and the demand for them determines the price charged by the T.V. networks.

As you read the article, think through why advertisers would pick the Super Bowl and also how the same considerations affect other companies' advertising choices. Also think how the need to appeal to advertisers and the desire for advertising revenue affects the choice of programming by T.V. companies.

Super Bowl ads cost megabucks

By Kathy Holub

SAN JOSE, Calif.—It happens only once a year: 38 million men line up on their living room couches, beer in one hand and cheese doodads in the other. They're boisterous, they're relaxed, they're what advertisers call festive. And they're all tuned to the same television channel at the same time.

No wonder the nation's premier vendors of beer, trucks and office equipment can't wait to beam sharp little messages into those captive brains on Super Bowl Sunday, January 20.

No wonder ABC-TV is getting away with charging $1 million (U.S.) this year for 60 seconds of commercial time, creating the most expensive television minute in history.

At least 16 major corporations and the U.S. Marines have snapped up Super Bowl ads so far, eager to reach the game's mammoth audience of 78 million – including roughly half the adult males in the United States.

"There's no better buy in the business," declares Cory Block, advertising account executive for Master Lock of Milwaukee.

Block should know. For the past 10 years the padlock manufacturer has bought only one national T.V. spot a year – a riveting 30-second ad on the Super Bowl,

to be played this year at Stanford Stadium.

The macho commerical shows a rifleman blasting a padlock to smithereens and then finding that the lock still holds. Most men in America, and many women, know that ad as well as their own phone numbers. In fact, 94 per cent of the public now knows the Master Lock name, Block says.

"Very few shows have more impact," he says. "It's a damn good way to reach men."

Devoted fans who resist the lures of bathroom and kitchen for six hours – from the start of the pregame show to the last post-game interview – will absorb at least 17 beer commercials (Anheuser-Busch, Miller and Stroh's), 17 car commercials (Nissan, Volkswagen and Ford), 14 ads for office equipment (IBM, Minolta, Sharp), three for hamburgers (McDonald's) and two for life insurance (Northwestern).

Dazzling audience

Almost 90 per cent of the ads have been sold so far, with IBM buying the most: one during the game and nine on the pregame show.

Anheuser-Busch, sensing a dazzling audience in the Super Bowl, has bought five ads during the game and three before kickoff. The centrepiece spot will be a 90-

second rhapsody on the company's commitment to quality, complete with Clydesdale horses.

Soloflex, the body-building system, bought one ad—presumably hoping to inspire 78 million couch potatoes to work off their beer flab with home exercise.

The U.S. Marines bought an ad, too, becoming the only sponsor to spend a hefty chunk of taxpayers' money. Like other sponsors, Marines spokesmen refuse to reveal how much they paid for the spot.

On a grimmer note, another male-oriented product is on the list, too: life insurance.

"We still gulp at that kind of money, but the Super Bowl has always done the job for us," says Robert Carboni, vice president of communications for Northwestern Mutual Life Insurance Co. of Milwaukee.

Most of the ads will last 30 seconds, a time period that ABC says it sells for $525,000. That's only a relative price, however. Some sponsors pay less by using seasoned negotiators and buying packages of ads – two Super Bowls, three Monday night footballs and six "Magnum P.I." ads, for example.

The exact time the spot airs affects the price, too. In general, the further way the spot is from kick-off, the less it costs. Pregame and postgame spots are cheaper than game spots.

In between, there's the prized "kickoff window."

Anheuser-Busch's 90-second beer poem will air in this window—the 15-minute time slot immediately before kickoff. Advertisers love the window because they know viewers' eyes are epoxied to the screen. Later, if the game is dull, fans may actually talk during the commercials, wander into the kitchen, get too drunk to understand English or—worst of all—turn the tube off.

Champagne glow

But that still doesn't explain why corporate sponsors pay so much for a few 30-second slivers of time.

For one thing, advertisers say the Super Bowl's effervescence lends a champagne glow even to the dullest products and the stodgiest companies.

They also say it makes them feel like members of an exclusive club. "Your fellow advertisers are vey high prestige companies. You like to be included in that," Carboni says.

The Toronto Star, Sunday, December 23, 1984, p. B1.

Concepts
to consider:

**Capitalism, economy,
influence, mass media,
persuasion.**

QUESTIONS

1. How many reasons can you think of for people to watch the Super Bowl on T.V.?

2. Why does advertising during the Super Bowl cost so much?

3. What happens to the money paid by advertisers to the T.V. network?

4. How easy or difficult do you think it would be to sell advertising spots during a T.V. documentary on, for example, child abuse or teen suicide? How might the need to attract advertisers influence the programme content?

5. "...the Super Bowl's effervescence lends a champagne glow even to the dullest products and the stodgiest companies." Explain this statement.

6. How do advertisers use the programme content and their knowledge of cultural norms and values in creating advertisements? Give examples— one from the article and one from your own watching of T.V.

7. Document the next programme you watch on T.V. Name the programme, summarize the programme's content, identify who the audience would be, and list the advertisers and their products. Briefly explain the connections between the programme, the products advertised, and the audience.

FIND A CLIPPING

Language is a symbolic system. Words have learned meanings, and through a judicious choice of words, meanings, images, and feelings can be created in readers' minds. Small changes in words can often alter the image and meaning. Newspapers use this knowledge of language to create an impact, and often a news report can be biased in a way that may not be apparent until you analyse the wording closely.

Find two, or more, newspaper or magazine reports on a group that has gained some notoriety or an event that has captured public attention. It would be interesting to compare a Canadian source and an American source reporting on the same subject.

Read each report carefully to see how objective the journalism is. Are the words used to describe people, ideas, or actions neutral words or are they "loaded"? Is the description of the events objective? Are all viewpoints given and is the presentation of all points of view balanced? Does the presentation reflect national interest? Does it reflect the interests of a particular social class or ethnic group?

Analyse and compare the reports carefully. Explain and give examples of the points you make.

5

Social Groups

A social group exists when a number of people interact with one another on the basis of shared expectations about each others' behaviour. People are in groups in their families, at work, in class, playing sports, going out with friends, partying, pursuing hobbies and interests, working for a political party, and so on. We are all involved in many different groups; in fact, it is hard to imagine life without meeting with others in group settings of various kinds. The nature and degree of our involvement varies. In primary groups, such as families or close friends, members have an emotional bond to one another such that the individual's place in that group can never be filled by another person. Each person is thought of as a unique individual bonded to others by family ties or close friendship and loyalties. In a primary group people can express their feelings and act spontaneously in ways that are not possible in the more formal setting of secondary groups.

Primary groups are considered the most important for a sense of emotional well-being, but secondary groups are generally more numerous in people's lives. Secondary groups are those formed for a purpose—they are goal oriented.

Members belong because of their interest in the group's goal, because of the contribution they can make towards achieving it, or because of the contribution group membership can make towards achieving their own goals (learning a new skill or earning an income, for example). School classes and work groups are both examples of a secondary group, as are church groups, sports clubs, political parties, a college newspaper office, and people at a party.

In a secondary group, members' actions are instrumental, being directed towards the purposes for which the group exists. Relations with others are more formal. Though friendships (primary group relations) may develop in a secondary group, they are not expected to interfere with working towards the group's goals. Role expectations guide relations with others in the group. Members can leave, and new members can join or be recruited to take their place.

The sociological concepts of status and role define the cultural prescriptions that indicate how people should act in the situations in which they find themselves. Status refers to the position: teacher, waiter, supervisor, doctor, politician, garbage man, student, Canadian, father, aunt, daughter, friend are examples of statuses which an individual may have. Each status usually carries a set of role expectations, the role being the part an individual is expected to play in a particular status. Social roles are analogous to the part written for an actor. Although in real life people put their own individual stamp on their roles, the role still constrains their actions. The role can be understood as a set of guidelines for a particular position. Most of the time familiar roles are taken on without a great deal of thought. Sometimes, however, unique situations arise that require individuals to create new roles, a situation that some people might find challenging, others somewhat threatening.

Belonging to a particular group may influence people's behaviour, expecially if they are concerned about being accepted by the other members and remaining part of the group. For example, when employees start a new job they are generally concerned that they do the work correctly, and often pay particular attention to how they dress and relate to others in order to make a good impression. Communication is facilitated through shared cultural knowledge of norms and involves tone of voice, facial expression, dress, gestures, body language, and use of space, all of which convey messages that are interpreted and understood because of the shared social meanings attached to them. Occasionally our interpretation or understanding of the situation proves wrong, and confusion or possibly embarassment, tensions, and misunderstandings follow.

The first article in this section is chosen to illustrate a characteristic of modern industrial society, the variety of group activities that are available through groups which are set up to meet people's needs and interests. Potential members hear about them via the mass media as well as by word of mouth, and so get the opportunity to meet others with similar interests. The second article deals with an innovative and increasingly popular form of housing—co-op housing, which requires some adjustments on the part of residents in return for the benefits. The third article deals with broken families, where relations have become very difficult and require the intervention of a third party.

What is Involved in Belonging to a Group?

INTRODUCTION

Sociologists label groups according to various characteristics of the relationships among the participants. Groups can, for example, be labelled primary groups, secondary groups, formal groups, informal groups, voluntary groups, involuntary groups, reference groups, or peer groups. Groups can be open or closed to new members, or open to certain people and closed to others. Groups may be long-lived or exist only for a short time. They may be independent or dependent on a larger parent organization. These categorizations serve to highlight the differing ways in which people can relate to one another within the group, and the extent of the commitment involved in that membership—or to put it another way, the variations in the rights and obligations of the group members to each other and to the group as a whole.

Many of the groups we belong to are secondary groups. The list of Nova Scotia events describes happenings that were being put on by various organizations in the Halifax area and which were open to members of the public. The questions that follow are designed to explore what is involved in belonging to groups, and also to highlight some of the ways in which we get to know other people. In answering the questions, consider either the group organizing the event, or the potential attenders, whichever is appropriate.

Nova Scotia Events

July-August—Afternoon teas, Thursdays, Weymouth Historical Society Building, 3-5 p.m. $2 adults, $1 children.

To Aug. 5—Exhibition of paintings by Judith Bartlet at The Dartmouth Heritage Museum Art Gallery. Info 421-2300/421-2199.

To Aug. 10—One week racquetball camps at the Dartmouth Sportplex. Monday to Friday, 9:30 a.m.-12 p.m. Pre-registration please. $20. Info 421-2600.

To Aug. 12—Mount Art Gallery exhibits: Halifax Storm Porches, by Renate Deppe, and CAR on the Road, by 30 Newfoundland artists. Info 443-4450.

To Sept. 1—Exhibits, Canadian coinage and N.S. silver, Public Archives of N.S., 6016 University Ave.

To Sept. 3—Brass Rubbing. Holy Trinity Church Hall, Middleton, 1-5 p.m.

To Sept. 9—Acquisitions 82-84, an Art Gallery of Nova Scotia exhibition on display in the Permanent Collection Gallery. Info 424-7542.

To Sept. 16—Aviation '84. A collection of artifacts relating to aviation will be on display at the Nova Scotia Museum, Summer St.

To Sept. 16—Bridgewater's DesBrisay Museum NEC exhibits: The Ox in Nova Scotia; postcard collection of Late George Penchard, scenes at early 20th century Lunenburg County.

July 27-30—Tennis lessons for August at the YWCA, Halifax. Beginner and intermediate. Info 423-6162.

July 27-30—Dartmouth Parks and Recreation Dept. will be conducting a user survey of all its parks and outdoor recreation facilities. Public support appreciated. Info 421-2307.

July 27-Aug. 10—Classes in dance, racquetball and swimming at the Dartmouth Sportplex. Info 421-2600.

July 27, 28—Red Cross craft sale, Bridgewater and South Shore malls 10 a.m.-10 p.m. weekdays 10 a.m.-4 p.m. Saturday. Info 423-9181, ext. 430.

July 27, 28—Centre Stage Theatre presents "Chapter Two" by Neil Simon 8:15 p.m. in the Cornwallis Inn, Kentville. $4/$3. Reservations 678-8040.

July 27-Aug. 5—Smokey Hollow Holidays. Country Harbour Gun Club, Country Harbour.

July 27—Poetry readings by N.S. writers, 8 p.m. Eyelevel Gallery, suite 306. Info 425-6412.

July 27—Notre Dame du Cap Choir. Shannon Park Recreation Centre 8:30 p.m. Info 422-2843.

Concepts to consider:

Aggregate, category, crowd, Gemeinschaft, Gesellschaft, group, mass media, primary group, secondary group.

July 27—Outdoor Jamboree. Upper Stewracke Elementary School, rain or shine. 8 p.m. $2.50/$1.

July 27—Home Baking Sale at Forrester's Hall, Maitland. Route 215. 10 a.m.-2 p.m.

July 27-28—Baddeck Handcraft Festival, Baddeck Fire Hall (daytime), Baddeck Rural High School on Friday evening. Info 295-3124.

July 27—Breakdance workshop at Dartmouth Sportsplex. 6:30-8:30 p.m. Ages 7-16 yrs. Pre-registration required. Info 421-2600.

July 27-29—Showing of Peter Seller's film, "Being There", National Film Board Theatre. 7-9:30 p.m. $3.

July 27-28—Halifax Dance Association variety show, Sir James Dunn Theatre. Friday 8 p.m. Saturday 2 p.m. and 8 p.m. $6/$5/$4. Info 422-2006.

July 27-29—Westphal District Horse Show. Robertson's Farm, West Lawrencetown, Halifax Co.

July 27-29—Lawrencetown, Halifax Co., presenting Fantasy Frolics Weekend. Fri., Monte Carlo, Sat. parade, dance, Sun. variety show.

July 28, 29—Collicutt Reunion, Cannaan, Route 14. Info 275-4487.

July 28-Aug. 26—The Shell Collectors Association of N.S. second annual exhibit, Maritime Museum of the Atlantic.

July 28-29—Africville's annual picnic at Fairview Cove entrance. 10:30 a.m. Church service 2 p.m. Sunday.

July 28—A Gift of Music, sponsored by Bahai of Cole Harbour, Black Cultural Centre. 1-3 p.m.

July 28—Family Fair, Sunset Adult Residential Centre, South Pugwash. 1-5 p.m.

July 28—St. John's Church Bazaar, Wallace. 10 a.m.-6 p.m. Seafood chowder and auction.

July 28—Lobster Supper, Salem, Church, River John. Noon. Info 351-2707.

July 28—'84 Open House and Alumni Reunion, N.S. Agricultural College, Truro, 11:30-4 p.m. Barbeque 11:30.

July 28—Lobster supper, St. Peter's Church Hall. Hackett's Cove. Hwy. 333. Cold ham for those who don't care for lobster. 4-7 p.m. $13/$7.

All notices for this column should be mailed or delivered at least 10 days prior to publication of the event to: Nova Scotia Events, P.O. Box 6710, Halifax, N.S., B3J 2T2.

The Chronicle-Herald, Halifax, Friday, July 27, 1984. Courtesy of The Chronicle-Herald and The Mail-Star.

QUESTIONS

1. Define social group. What distinguishes a group from a crowd, aggregate or a category of people?

2. In sociological terms, list all the different types of groups you can think of. Use a text book or lecture notes.

3. Take two examples from the list in the article. What kind of groups would these be to their members? What kind of group would they be to outsiders?

4. What kinds of groups are not represented in this list? Why are they not represented?

5. What events are children or teenagers likely to go to? Are young people's social worlds different from that of adults? Explain the difference.

6. Why are the details of the groups' meetings printed in the newspaper? How else could people hear about these events?

7. If you planned on attending one of the Nova Scotia Events listed, would you know roughly what to expect, what to wear, and how to act? Discuss what your expectations would be if you attended one event on the list. How would you know?

8. Could you survive in society without belonging to any social group?

9. Identify all the groups you have participated in for the past week. What type of group was each?

How Residents Have to Adapt to Housing Arrangement

INTRODUCTION

This article suggests that living in co-operative housing requires special adjustments on the part of residents. Equally complex adjustments are probably required in other housing arrangements, such as senior citizens' apartment blocks, housing for the handicapped, exclusive private developments, student housing, and so on.

One way to appreciate why co-operative living arrangements might require "a special kind of person" is to compare them with more usual forms of housing such as in suburbia, in apartment blocks, or housing in small towns. These provide residents with a degree of privacy that co-op housing does not. Housing arrangements which are in some way unusual will have a less clear set of guidelines (norms) for getting along with fellow residents. Co-operative housing requires people to interact and to co-operate in running the housing complex. This provides benefits to the residents but it will also pose challenges or raise problems because not all residents are equally willing or able to become involved in the required work.

The first residents will probably establish some norms and later residents will fit into these, accepting the normative patterns already established in the housing complex. If they cannot adapt they may move out, or work to change the way things are done.

Co-op dwellers special kind of people

By Susan Gillen
Gillen is a Saskatoon freelance writer.

It takes a special kind of person to fit into the co-operative living environment, Terra resident Barbara Millsap says.

Other members of the city's first co-operative housing development agree, including Thom Armstrong, who finds it socially and economically rewarding, and Pat Davis, who found its demands overwhelming.

Moving to Saskatoon about a year ago, Millsap looked for "a way to meet people, and an area with lots of kids for ours to play with." She found both at Terra. The complex of 48 townhouses encloses a large "green space" for socializing, a community building for numerous meetings, and an adventure playground for the children.

"If you want contact with others you just hang around this centre space," Millsap said, noting that "others" include about 80 adults and 70 children. Mothers at home with preschoolers ran a weekly indoor playground program in the centre last winter, and plan to do it again.

"We watch out for each other... if parents aren't home when kids come home from school, they don't hesitate to go to a neighbor, and we always have someone nearby to call on in an emergency. You have to be willing to give up some privacy to have those benefits."

Co-op dwellers learn to become tolerant of all kinds of people from a wide variety of educational, economic and ethnic backgrounds, she said. "If you're painting the fence right beside someone's house you get to know them."

Residents note that problems in new co-op housing can mean a couple of rocky years in the beginning. Some find the rewards less than expected, or the obligations of maintenance and meetings too much for them. While Saskatchewan people have not yet grasped the concept, which is new here, co-ops elsewhere in Canada have two- and three-year waiting lists.

Terra resident Armstrong feels that while the concept is not easy to work, it's worth the effort. "We're not brought up to co-operate. Our economic system teaches us to get things at the expense of others, so a lot of us don't have the practice at community living. Older people who grew up in small towns have those ties. People my age are a generation of renters."

Problems reach their peak in the first year of co-operative living, as residents need time to develop skills for management, maintenance and conflict resolution. Coping mechanisms include bylaw committees, grievance procedures and educational programs, as well as a lot of peer pressure. Simple confrontation can often defuse a conflict.

Citing the need for confidentiality guidelines, Armstrong said that dealing with a person in a combination of ways—friend, neighbor and business partner—can jeopardize privacy. Some tend to feel that everybody knows too much about them, he said.

Committees meet frequently, and all members must attend a monthly meeting. The children have also picked up on the idea of group decisions, and hold meetings on such concerns as playground equipment. Even four year-olds have their hands up.

With costs held down by voluntary maintenance, residents contribute according to their skills. "Planners" feel comfortable with frequent meetings and organizational problems, while "doers" may offer typing, plumbing or painting skills.

"We build a support system for each other—that's the key to the whole thing," Armstrong said. He finds that living in a real community environment for the first time in his adult life more than compensates for the difficulties.

On the other hand, Pat Davis found the demands of co-operative living "somewhat exhausting, especially the emphasis on meetings." Preparing to leave Terra for a house of her own, Davis noted that her job included a lot of after-hour work commitments and committee work, and she tended to feel "'meeting-ed' out." "You can easily become overwhelmed by it," she said.

Davis expressed further frustration at what she considered an inequitable sharing of maintenance tasks. She felt that some carried a bare minimum workload while a committed and conscientious core

Concepts to consider:

Conformity, definition of the situation, group, in-group, interaction, involuntary group, out-group, peer group, peer pressure, personal space, primary group, role, secondary group, social pressure, voluntary group.

group picked up the slack. "I was in that core group and I wanted it to work," she said.

With a high-pressure, people-oriented job, Davis cherishes her privacy and time alone. "If you go out in the green space, you're part of that community and open for communication all the time . . . but you might just want to have a beer and read a book."

Emphasizing that her six-month stay at Terra was a learning experience rather than a bad experience, Davis concluded: "People who fit will stay, and the co-operative will work."

Star-Phoenix, Saskatoon, Saturday, June 9, 1984, p. D1.

QUESTIONS

1. Describe the role of "co-op dwellers" in this housing complex. Use the article plus you own insights.

2. How does this role differ from that of a suburban resident or resident in a small town?

3. What are the goals of co-op housing?

4. Do the co-op dwellers described in this article constitute a secondary group?

5. How are residents of co-op housing selected? Are they a voluntary group or an involuntary group? How will this affect the way people participate in running the housing co-operative?

6. Approximately how many people are involved in this co-op housing complex? What would you judge to be the age range? How does this demographic composition affect interaction within the group?

7. How exactly can conformity to social norms be imposed on residents in co-op housing — or can it?

8. How might "personal space" be established temporarily for a resident on the public "green space"?

9. What measures could be used to safeguard against long-stay tenants forming an in-group and making new residents feel like outsiders? Or would it matter if old-timers did form an in-group?

Breakup of the Primary Group

INTRODUCTION

The family is the primary group often viewed as the foundation of emotional well-being. If the family group is broken by divorce or separation, individuals have to work out new relationships with ex-spouse and children at a time when it may be exceedingly difficult to do so without great emotional turmoil.

The response to separation or divorce is obviously very individualized. However, social factors do have considerable influence. Cultural values relating to family life, and the roles family members should play, are socially defined and are internalized. They serve as a kind of script on which individual performance is based. The breaking of these familial roles when the family splits up can be accompanied by much anger, bitterness, and unhappiness. The role of ex-husband or ex-wife is, by contrast with the married role, not clearly defined, and the absence of social guidelines makes relations difficult, since new roles have to be created by the parties concerned. Where the family break-up is preceeded by considerable conflict or violence, post-separation interaction may be very acrimonious. A third-party mediator may be necessary when family members meet.

As you answer the questions, consider how social prescriptions influence individuals and guide even their most intimate relationships with others, and think about the converse—the anguish and emotional turmoil that result from broken relationships and the lack of social norms to mediate them.

Divorced parents visit children under supervised conditions

TORONTO (CP)—In cases where there is bitterness and hostility between separated or divorced parents, where visits with the children cause tension and strife, and where custody itself may be a contentious issue, family court and community agencies have long been unable to achieve a breakthrough.

But Access for Parents and Children in Ontario, which began in 1981, has proved to be the answer to what one judge has described as an "insoluble problem."

The project offers parents who don't have custody of their children a chance to see them under supervised conditions.

Access offers a neutral, conflict-free atmosphere in which parent and child can enjoy happy, constructive contact.

"They enjoy the time together with each other," said project director Noreen Musclow. "The kids feel some shyness at first, but they are reassured to see other kids in the same situation."

In the past year alone, more than 115 families used the program which runs Saturday mornings and Sunday afternoons at a facility in suburban Etobicoke that provides a variety of community services.

It was the core staff at the Lakeshore Area Multi-Service Project and Etobicoke family court Judge F. Stewart Fisher—after seeing more and more situations in which families required a third party to intervene in disputes involving visits—who urged the establishment of Access.

Musclow, a registered nurse with degrees in psychology and special education who used to work in the psychiatry department at Toronto General Hospital, was asked to run the program.

She immediately set out to find funding, getting a $14,500 grant from the United Church of Canada and $3,000 from Met-

Concepts to consider:

Conjugal family, formal organization, primary group, role, romantic love, secondary group, social institution, social interaction, values, voluntary organization.

ropolitan Toronto Community and Social Services. This year, Access received an $18,000 grant from the United Church and $3,000 from the city of Etobicoke.

The custodial parent takes the child to the centre at a prearranged time and waits in a separate room while the child and the non-custodial parent play with toys and games in the community room.

Either Musclow, a social worker, summer student or a volunteer worker is present during the visit.

On a typical Sunday, there are eight to 10 non-custodial parents visiting with their children.

Eighty per cent of the visits are court-directed from family courts in Etobicoke, Brampton and Toronto. The service is also used by parents from Hamilton, Orangeville and other parts of the province.

The London Free Press, Monday, July 23, 1984, p. D2.

QUESTIONS

1. What are the characteristics of a primary group?

2. Are children and non-custodial parents a primary group?

3. What exactly has happened to the primary group ties that can make contact between non-custodial parents and their children so difficult and tension-ridden?

4. What are the characteristics of a secondary group?

5. Is Access a secondary group? Explain why. What are its goals?

6. How are Access staff and volunteers able to achieve these goals? Consider their training, motivation, and relationship to the clients.

7. What theoretical perspective would provide the best framework for researching the problem of friction in broken families?

FIND A CLIPPING

Find a clipping that clearly focuses on a social group. Discuss the activities of this group. Is this group a primary or secondary group? Explain your choice. What is the purpose, or goal, of this group (for example, is it friendship, business, religious)?

Define what is meant by social roles. What are the social roles mentioned in your clipping? Are any roles more important than others? (If so, explain why.) Are any members of this group experiencing role strain or role conflict? If they are, explain why this strain or conflict is occurring.

To what other groups might members of the group you are discussing belong?

6

Formal Organizations

A major share of the work in an industrial society is achieved by formal organizations (or complex organizations as they are commonly called). Formal organizations are secondary groups deliberately and rationally desiged to achieve a specific goal. Formal organizations bring together people who are strangers to one another and enable their skills and labour to be co-ordinated so that their combined efforts serve the goals of the organization. The process of formalization guides and regulates human conduct in organizations so that spontaneity is largely controlled and employees' performance becomes predictable.

Bureaucracy, in everyday usage, is a derogatory term. In fact, as a mode of organizing work it is extremely effective. The characteristics of bureaucracy within a large organization, to summarize Max Weber, include a hierarchy of authority, a division of labour, and rules and guidelines to co-ordinate the activities of many specialized staff members. Staff are appointed, and promoted, according to their qualifications to do specified tasks. Record keeping is important. Clients are treated in an impersonal manner according to rules, not according to their individual characteristics.

The above describes the structure and workings of formal organizations. However, in any formal organization informal modes of operating come into being between employees. Understandings, agreed-upon ways of operating, short cuts, ways of covering up for others, develop in networks of employees. These informal methods of co-operating usually make working life easier and more pleasant for employees.

Because work takes up a large portion of daily life, social relationships with other employees are important; these provide a personal dimension to work. Many people make friends (form primary relationships) at work, and this obviously makes their work lives that much more enjoyable. A workplace where relations between staff are unfriendly usually has low morale, poor productivity and, if employment conditions permit, a high turnover of staff.

Organizations operate within a social context and, therefore, any organization must take account of its environment. An open-systems model of organizations draws attention to the economic, political, cultural and physical context within which any organization works, and to the outside influences that impinge upon its operations.

Social Control in the Workplace

INTRODUCTION

One of the characteristics of formal organizations is that the behaviour of staff is controlled while they are at work, at least in as far as their actions relate to the goals of the organization. The concepts of formalization, authority, status, and role capture this idea. While people's performance at work can be made relatively predictable, this certainly does not mean it is totally controlled. There are limits to the authority and to the influence that can be exercised over employees in the workplace. Managers and supervisors have to recognize these limits and yet must achieve good interpersonal relations between their workers in the interests of productivity and a pleasant working environment. As this article illustrates, some behaviour is hard to control... and may become a significant problem.

Nasty habits can ruin office morale

By Helen Bullock

Is work hazardous to your mental health?

Employees rightly worry about dangerous chemicals, uncomfortable furniture, lighting levels, noise and radiation, but one of the most dangerous and unpleasant things in the work environment can be other people.

They bring to work personal habits that conflict with yours. And one or two workers with destructive habits can ruin an entire working atmosphere.

As funny as it may sound to call the chain-smoking supervisor, "Smokestack" behind his back, an employee relations counsellor explains: "A sensitive person surrounded by people whose habits are intolerable will soon be a nervous wreck.

"They suppress their annoyance, which becomes anger and hostility. They become nervous and irritated and, more importantly to the company, unproductive."

A big complaint, of course, is smoking.

Smokers and non-smokers are pitted against each other in a fight to the finish.

Some consolation

It may be some consolation to think that, statistically, smokers will be finished years earlier than their non-smoking co-workers.

But smokers insist on their right to have a cigarette at their desk if it soothes them, helps them concentrate and they enjoy it. No laws or bylaws, only courtesy prevents a smoker from lighting up in large offices.

Management occasionally passes an in-house rule forbidding smoking in office areas, "but they don't have much luck with it," admits John Keays of the Ontario health ministry,"We don't keep statistics on the number of companies who try this, but we get some feedback and I can tell you it's not many."

Keays says a new law passed recently in San Francisco makes it possible for a non-smoker to request a non-smoking work area, but he hasn't yet heard how it is being put into action.

Anne Moon, spokesman for the Toronto health department, says a city investigator is just back from San Francisco and is writing a report for the city's legal and medical departments on the possibilities of a smokefree workplace.

Matter of logistics

But it is often a matter of logistics. If an office has six smokers and one non-smoker, pushing his or her desk off into a corner isn't going to give much relief.

It's still questionable whether second-hand smoke is harmful to non-smokers although evidence suggests that a lungful of someone else's poison can also poison you.

Businesses do strive for solutions. They ask employees to refrain from excessive smoking, provide separate lounges for smokers and non-smokers and have non-smoking sections of the staff cafeteria. They install good ventilation systems and air purifiers, although their effect is "psychological in value largely," according to John Keays quoting recent studies.

Courtesy seems the only hope.

But no legislation can deal with troubling personal problems such as hygiene.

Ann Crocker, a former administrative assistant now freelancing from home, recalls she once worked in a medium-sized printing and graphics company where the boss's problem was overwhelming.

"He had appalling body odor," Crocker recalls. "One woman staffer brought air freshener sticks in to keep on her desk."

She and other employees frequently discussed confronting the boss but nobody had the nerve to risk losing a job.

One girl finally had a word with the boss's wife but with no re-sults. The wife was affronted and the husband remained unbathed.

"It was difficult because he was the boss," Crocker said. "But his appearance and odor certainly cost the company clients."

Eventually somebody has to bell the cat, whether the offender is boss or employee. Employee counsellors say that deteriorating hygiene and poor grooming may be a warning sign, indicating depression and mental stress. The offending employee may need professional help.

Tackle the problem

If the company has an on-site health centre, one of its staff might counsel the offender, using a "medical" approach that will keep things neutral and keep personalities out of it. If not, it's up to the immediate supervisor or manager to tackle the problem head on.

Counsellors suggest that if the employee deals with the public, it may be possible to use a tactful approach along the line of "now you're meeting more people, the company feels you'd be more effective if you dressed this way...," indicating that grooming is an issue of concern.

If the employee is deskbound, the manager might as well be blunt. Says one counsellor, "They should approach the employee just as they would if the problem was lateness for work or poor quality work. The complaint must be dealt with on a professional level, not as a personal slur."

Co-worker irritants come in many other shapes and sounds.

Number 1 on a host of lists is gum-chewing. The snap, smack and pop of a veteran chewer is torture to a sensitive soul, as is knuckle-cracking, excessive throat clearing, nail and teeth picking and humming.

Managers are usually reluctant to tackle these problems because at first glance they seem petty and trivial. But they should face them before they have a major morale problem.

An employee who has only half his mind on his work while the other half frets, "if that guy doesn't stop that I'll go crazy," is not a productive employee.

Management can do its bit by facing the offenders and the problem openly, sensibly and sympathetically.

Employees can do their bit by being courteous and considering the comfort of others.

And the offenders can *cut it out*.

The Toronto Star, Wednesday, April 4, 1984, p. C2.

Concepts to consider:

Authority, formal organization, informal organization, norms, role performance, sanctions, secondary group, social control, social interaction, status.

QUESTIONS

1. What are the characteristics of a formal organization? Are the work settings described in the article found in formal organizations?

2. On what basis are people hired to work for a company?

3. What is the nature and boundaries of the authority exercised in a formal organization by the boss or supervisors?

4. What sort of authority or influence can be exercised over people by co-workers? What are the limits to these forms of control?

5. Are the "nasty habits" mentioned in the article a problem to the company, to the people who are bothered by them, or both. Explain the problems.

6. What solutions can you suggest to the problems you outlined above? Use those suggested in the article or your own ideas. Focus on the work environment and explain why you think the solution you propose would be successful.

7. Identify ways in which other students annoy you in the classroom. What solutions are there to these problems? Who has the authority or influence to deal with them? What are the constraints on this authority or influence?

8. If you had to study the relations between workers in an office setting, what theoretical perspective would you use as a framework for your research? Explain why briefly.

The Impact of Organization on Personal Service

INTRODUCTION

Nursing homes are one way to provide care to the dependent elderly. If they are run for profit, there is a potential conflict between the goals of making a profit and providing good service. The following report deals with this specific issue.

There are alternatives for providing care for those over 65 years and in need. But since it is impossible to put the whole responsibility onto families, services will continue to be channelled through formal organizations of various types. The questions that follow are designed to make you think about the impact of the structure and internal dynamics of the various organizations on the quality of service.

Outlaw private personal care homes, study group urges

By Jane Armstrong

TORONTO (CP)—A crackdown on nursing homes is urgently needed in light of widespread horror stories about the mistreatment of the elderly, a report commissioned by the Canadian Medical Association said.

"The standard of care provided in many nursing homes is grossly inadequate," said the report released last week.

"They provide a life of immobility and tedium and lack any guarantee of adequate basic care."

In the short term, strict standards must be imposed and enforced, the report said.

In the long run, governments should eliminate all nursing homes run privately for profit and establish a system of publicly financed and operated institutions.

"Permitting nursing homes to be run for profit under a lenient system of legislation and an impotent system of inspection is a measure of societal negligence we can no longer allow to continue," the study said.

Joan Watson, chairman of the five-person group which held public hearings across the country, said there were many poignant presentations which highlighted shortcomings in the nursing home field.

A brief by the Concerned Friends of Ontario Citizens in Care Facilities Inc. said some institutions are cockroach-infested, don't provide nutritious meals or enough baths, monitor mail and phone conversations and keep the doors locked.

Some nursing homes are "sterile, friendless and lacking in humanness and warmth, where old people sit and rock, stare at the walls for most of the day, or are led around by the hand like small children by inadequately enlightened staff who refer to them as 'dear,'" said the brief, which is quoted at length in the study group's report.

Other briefs stressed the lack of properly trained staff in some nursing homes.

"If Canadian society were judged by the way it treats its elderly, it would be found wanting," Watson, former host of the CBC-TV consumer affairs show *Marketplace*, told a news conference.

The nursing home system in Ontario, for example, is "disgusting," she said. "It is just not in any way a credit to the Ontario government."

She said the level of care varied from province to province and

52

Ontario was not necessarily the worst but was the one with which the study group had the most experience.

The group emphasized the need to get elderly people out of institutions, expecially in light of projections that Canada's aging population is going to cause gargantuan increases in health-care costs.

Perhaps 13 per cent of the population will be 65 or older by the turn of the century, a figure that could rise to 18.2 per cent—almost double the 1981 rate of 9.7 per cent—by the year 2021, the study said.

"If we continue to put old people in institutions at the rate we do now, the costs will not only be prohibitive, we will perpetuate the callous practice of warehousing the elderly."

The study said changes in the makeup of the population alone could increase health care expenditures within the next 40 years by about 75 per cent to more than $32 billion.

Thousands more hospital and long-term care beds will be needed unless lower-cost alternatives involving home and community care are developed.

Among the support services which the study group said should be more readily available to allow the elderly to stay at home or live with relatives are: public health nurses, meals on wheels, companions, homemakers, handyman programs, drop-in centres and hospitals where consumers can get medical care without being admitted overnight.

While there will always be some people who will have to stay in institutions, the study said, there should be enough flexibility in the system to let them move from one level of care to another.

Nursing homes, for example, provide higher levels of nursing care than homes for the aged. It said assessment services should be set up to evaluate residents' needs and make sure they are being met.

The group said New Brunswick has had great success with an experimental "extra-mural" hospital, a mobile unit which goes to patients' homes to provide health care in their bedrooms.

This way, hospital admissions are shortened or avoided, the terminally ill can be treated at home and admissions to nursing homes can be postponed.

Brandon Sun, Monday, August 20, 1984, p. 14. With permission of The Canadian Press.

Concepts to consider:

Formalization, formal organization, organizational goals, pressure group, primary groups, power, secondary groups, voluntary groups.

QUESTIONS

1. Explain why a nursing home can be regarded as a formal organization.

2. Do the structure and the goals of profit-oriented formal organizations work against providing for friendliness, support, affection, respect and similar sentiments that clients would enjoy?

3. If some nursing homes are as inadequate as this newspaper report suggests, why don't patients or others complain?

4. Is it likely that publicly financed and operated nursing homes would offer better care? Explain why you answer as you do.

5. Why can families not be held totally responsible for caring for the elderly?

6. List the other solutions suggested for caring for the population over 65 years who need assistance.

7. Are these services to be provided by formal organizations? Explain how each would help in meeting the goal of humane service to the elderly.

8. Politicians are bombarded with requests for new programmes that require funding from taxation. How would you reduce the cost of a needed government-run service to care for the elderly?

9. Precisely who can bring pressure on the government to get a particular service for the elderly started? How can they influence government?

FIND A CLIPPING

Some organizations try deliberately to exclude outside influences. The concept of total institution is used to describe bureaucratically organized settings which attempt to monitor and control all aspects of life for those within its boundaries. A prison, mental hospital or a monastery are examples.

Find a clipping that relates to a total institution. Drawing on the clipping, your knowledge of formal organizations, and your imagination, describe the impact this closed setting would have on (a) social relationships between the inmates or residents, (b) between the inmates or residents and the paid staff, and (c) between the inmates or residents and their friends or family.

Socialization

Socialization is the learning process through which individuals develop their personalities and gain a sense of identity. It is also the process by which individuals are integrated into their society through learning the culture and participating in social life.

Socialization is a life-long process, but the key period is childhood, when primary socialization takes place. During the time they are growing up, children learn the culture and lifestyle of their own particular group; their ethnic background, religion, social class, environment, and experiences all profoundly influence the content and pattern of their socialization.

Learning and adaptation continues throughout life (adult or secondary socialization), building on the primary socialization of childhood. Secondary socialization in adult life is necessary because of the number, range, and complexity of the roles adults are required to play; because many people are mobile both socially and geographically; and because of the rapid pace of social change which makes much of childhood learning out of date.

The process of socializing young children in-volves many people and organizations. Sociologists refer to those who actually do the teaching and role modelling to children as the "agents of socialization." Agents of socialization are the individuals or organizations who pass on the culture of the group. Four agents are commonly singled out for special attention: the family, especially parents, school, peers, and the mass media. The family is considered to be the key influence, but the others are also important. Two agents of socialization, the family and the school, have a clear social mandate to inculcate the culture into children. The influence of peer groups and the mass media is more subtle and diffuse, but nevertheless they, too, can influence how the individual understands and responds to the social environment.

The first two articles in this section explore some of the experiences of childhood, the impact of different settings for socialization, and the influence of fads and fashions on children. The last article examines one area where the position of women has changed and where previous socialization needs to be overcome to enable women to take advantage of new opportunities.

Day Care or Home Care?

INTRODUCTION

The two letters reproduced here appeared in the same issue of Homemaker's Magazine in response to an earlier article on day care (May 1984). Homemaker's is distributed free to over 1,300,000 homes in preselected areas of 28 Canadian cities. The distribution is to target households with disposable incomes of interest to the advertisers.

Parents have the prime responsibility for the care of their children who are still legal minors. However, when parents work outside the home the care of pre-school children and of young school-aged children is a problem. Parents work for a variety of reasons; single parents work out of economic necessity; many two-parent families need the two incomes to lift the family above the poverty line. Some women are reluctant to take years out of the workforce for child raising, fearing to lose a career they have worked hard to establish.

These letter writers recognize that all care-givers have contributed to the socialization process; their underlying concern is that the context (home or day care) affects the content. The second writer quite obviously feels that a mother's care is superior in content to any day care. You should consider whether this is necessarily true.

In thinking about the questions, focus on the purpose of socialization, what can and what cannot be offered in alternative settings, and the constraints on achieving whatever is seen as the desired alternative.

A Matter of Priorities

Madam:

Your article *The Crisis in Day Care* (May '84) hit home. We were recently placed in the position of having to find day care for our four-year-old within an 18-day period when the day-care centre he was in closed. The alternatives my husband and I viewed at that time staggered us, so radically varied were the conditions and standards of care. Considering that children are our future, why are there no government programs to regulate and standardize these vitally important facilities?

With the pressure we were under to find good alternative day care, we quickly learned what to look for (and what not to look for). We were fortunate, but I shudder to think of what those parents less fortunate than we were have to go through to get good day care. Who needs a domed stadium for all those millions when a social need such as this exists?

L.R./Toronto, Ontario

Help Mothers Stay Home

...Many mothers who are home struggling on one income feel angry that their husbands are being taxed more and more to pay for other people's children in day care. No one is forced to be a mother, and if some women feel that they cannot give a child a mere five years out of their three-score and ten, then they shouldn't bother. Governments should be helping mothers stay home and look after their children properly, and families should be prepared to sacrifice material acquisitions in exchange for a lasting relationship with their child. If you want to be a mother then do the job properly—don't pass the responsibility over to the rest of us!

R.M./Thornhill, Ontario

Homemaker's Magazine July/August 1984, p. 114.

Concepts to consider:

Agents of socialization, conflict theory, day care, family, formal organization, functionalism, mass media, primary group, primary socialization, role, secondary group, values, work.

QUESTIONS

1. Why do parents go to work? List all the reasons you can think of for fathers and mothers to work outside the home.

2. Explain the difference between a primary group and a secondary group. Which concept applies to a family, and which to a day care centre?

3. What does a child cared for at home receive that cannot be provided in day care? (In answering this question, do not assume that all families are two-parent families or have stable, loving relationships.)

4. What does a child in day care get that cannot be provided easily at home?

5. In the first letter, the writer is concerned about the lack of regulation and standardization of day care programmes. Are regulation and standardization necessary? Explain why or why not.

6. In the second letter, the writer says, "Governments should be helping mothers stay home . . . ." In what ways could the government help mothers stay home? Would helping mothers stay home meet the needs you listed for question (1)?

7. Why shouldn't fathers be helped to stay home? What problems might arise in trying to implement such a policy?

8. Look at your answers to questions (5), (6), and (7). Identify the social values you applied in answering these questions.

9. If you were to analyse the relationships between families with young children, the work world and day care, would a functionalist analysis be an appropriate framework? Explain why, or why not.

10. Opinions on whether day care places should be provided and publicly funded vary widely. What social factors are likely to influence the opinions of readers of Homemaker's Magazine?

The Impact of Fashion Fads on Children

INTRODUCTION

The influences on children as they grow are many. It is unclear just how much children do learn from each of the diverse cultural pressures to which they are subjected. Some experiences children encounter have an impact on their learning, other experiences have less of an impact, depending on the age/stage the child has reached, the nature of the experience, and the people involved.

Trends in the youth culture are spread rapidly via the media. Most children and young people spend hours daily watching T.V. and listening to radio. Just how much impact the media has on children's learning and their perception of the world is difficult to establish but the media, particularly T.V., are definitely very important.

Parents are usually reckoned to be the most important agents of socialization. However, parents themselves are subject to considerable pressure to conform to cultural fads and fashions in lifestyles both for themselves and their children.

Parents may veto some of the things their children would like to have or would like to do, but they cannot filter all their children's experiences. The article that follows discusses some conflicting opinions on the effect of one fad upon children.

Opinions vary on children's 'camo'

VANCOUVER (CP)—Children are wearing jumpsuits, T-shirts, jackets, combat pants, shorts and peaked hats—all in the camouflage pattern and styles worn by United States marines in Vietnam and Central America.

"As a mother of three children, I'm really disturbed by it," says Susan Hargraves, a graduate student in educational psychology at Simon Fraser University. "I've observed boys dressed in camouflage playing at my son's after-school day care and at the housing co-op where we live. They fantasize about war and pretend they are soldiers."

The clothing is planting subtle seeds in children's minds that will make war seem acceptable, she says.

But an expert in popular culture says it's just another fashion trend.

Martin Laba, a communications professor at Simon Fraser University, says the trend began when the rock band The Clash wore camouflage as a political statement against U.S. military policy in Central America.

The popularity of the clothing shows how a symbol starts out with a certain significance, but loses meaning once it is appropriated by the rest of society, he says.

"It's not a fascination with military things or a symptom of increased militarism in society—absolutely not," says Laba.

He says it is an example of the "moral panic" that has been around since rock and roll music appeared—the feeling of adults that children's morals will be negatively affected by popular trends.

Some parents refuse to buy the clothes—made small enough to fit a two-year-old—because of its connotations of war. And store clerks say those parents who do buy it often tell them they dislike the clothes but are buying them because the child wants them.

Ari Feder, 12, says he wears camouflage because it's the style. For him, the trend started with Mr. T. in the popular television show, *The A-Team*, in which Mr. T. plays a Vietnam war veteran as a modern-day guerrrrilla who fights evil. Ari's proud of the fact his shirt is "a replica of genuine army stock," but says he doesn't play war.

Bill Tombrink cringed when he saw the camouflage outfit displayed on a stealthily crouching model in Woodward's boys' wear department and the racks bursting with the stuff.

"I wore the same thing for the German navy in Russia 40 years ago," said Tombrink. "I feel this is the same thing as the Hitler Youth, only on a different scale .... The kids don't know why they're wearing it, but it's like it was then—every kid had to have it."

Fatigues or G.I. Joe clothes, as children call them, were first sold only at army surplus outlets, but

now are available in department stores.

Lee Kirkby, a buyer for Woodward's boys' wear, says rather than being introduced by the department store and gaining popularity, the clothes were ordered after continuing demand from children.

Ali Motevaselan, owner of Camouflage, a military clothing shop that sells "camo" to both adults and children, says military clothing has always had a following among children.

"Kids always like anything to do with the military. They like war movies and guns. They like to look like a military man. They feel like they're big then."

The Sun-Times, Owen Sound, Monday, August 20, 1984, p. 5. With permission of The Canadian Press.

Concepts to consider:

Agents of socialization, culture, economy, fads, mass media, peer group, role playing, socialization, symbol, symbolic interaction.

QUESTIONS

1. Explain what is meant by socialization.

2. Define and explain symbolic interaction.

3. Who or what teaches children the meaning of symbols?

4. Is clothing a symbol? Why do children and adolescents want to wear camouflage clothing?

5. "Moral panic" is defined in the article. Why might parents experience "moral panic"?

6. Who buys camouflage clothing? What influences these people to buy it? (Use the article and your own experience.) What role has the media played in instigating the desire for camouflage clothing?

7. What short- and long-term impact do you think camouflage clothing would have on children's view of war? Would it likely be the same for all? Explain why the impact might vary.

8. Consult your textbook on any one of the many theories that describe the growth stages of children (such as Erickson, Mead, Piaget, Freud). Select one theorist and state at which stage you think the wearing of camouflage clothing would have the most lasting impression on a child.

Adult Socialization for Changing Roles

INTRODUCTION

Generally, women have been under-represented in those positions involving decision making. This is now changing gradually. Women's groups have argued for promoting many more women to positions that provide opportunities to exercise power and influence. It can also be argued that further changes in the status of women in society cannot be achieved unless women are involved in greater numbers in politics. This article focuses on one particular attempt to increase the participation of women in politics.

Sex roles learned in the process of growing up will often have to be revised in adult life. In a complex world, adult socialization is becoming increasingly important. This process is necessary to equip people for the undertaking of new roles, working in non-traditional occupations, and adapting to changing social values.

Day-long seminar aims to get women into politics

By Eileen Morrow

WHY NOT me?

That's the question the Hamilton Status of Women Committee wants to ask themselves this year when local elections roll around.

The Hamilton committee is encouraging local women to get involved in politics. To help promote that goal, it's offering a seminar on Saturday, May 29, on how to run for office and what to do when you get there.

This may be the year Hamilton sees a number of women take to the hustings, according to Irene Stayshyn, committee chairman and member of the Canadian Council on the Status of Women.

And it's about time, too.

"Look at our city hall. How many women do we have there?" asks Miss Stayshyn. "We don't have any. And I think for our city to make anything of itself, it will have to have women's ideas."

But women planning to run for office will face problems, she admits.

Traditionally, when women are involved in political activity, they're relegated to the back room. And lack of confidence in themselves tends to keep them there.

Miss Stayshyn says women need to recognize their abilities and shake off feelings that they're not prepared for political life.

"Maybe we're not prepared but that doesn't mean we can't change and get in there."

Both women and men may be turned off political campaigning because they think it takes a lot of money. But that's not necessarily true, says Miss Stayshyn.

She estimates the total cost of a local ward campaign at about $700.

"If you are willing to go out there and do everything yourself with your friends, the only things you have to worry about are signs and brochures."

The times are right for women to get into politics, explains Miss Stayshyn.

The women's movement has made the public and political parties aware of the imbalance of men to women in political office, she says, and all sectors are trying to set things right.

On the other hand, women shouldn't expect an easy ride. They have to be prepared to work hard.

She advises women to "work

hard, be yourself, and don't underestimate yourself."

Women who are interested in politics should become involved in organizations, service clubs, PTA associations or any group where they can show their concern for the local area, she says.

And aspiring female politicians should know thoroughly and openly express their opinions on local issues, she adds.

"The more outside contacts you have, the more people you have to choose from to help you reach your goal."

While she recommends that women get as much support from other women as they can, Miss Stayshyn doesn't suggest they run strictly on women's issues.

"I don't think women should run on a feminist platform. They should run on all the issues. They're going to be there to represent both men and women, young and old."

Practical considerations aside, women need to have a strong emotional make-up to survive in the political world.

Practical advice

They should be able to make decisions, stand up under pressure and slough off self-doubts and fear of the unknown.

"You have to have lots of guts," says Miss Stayshyn.

Speakers at the day-long seminar will try to give women the confidence and practical advice they need to take the plunge into politics.

Regional Chairman Anne Jones, Mayor Betty Ward, Alderperson Anne Reddish and School Trustee June Deans will be among the presenters.

The seminar runs from 9 a.m. to 4 p.m., Saturday, May 29, at Mohawk College, Fennel Campus.

The Hamilton Spectator, Saturday, May 15, 1982, p. 27.

Concepts to consider:

Adult socialization, agents of socialization, gender role, gender socialization, political participation, politics, primary socialization, resocialization, voluntary organization.

QUESTIONS

1. Why have so few women run for political office in the past? List those reasons given in the article plus any other reasons that you can think of.

2. Look at the reasons you have listed. Are they related to the way women are socialized as children and adults, systematic discrimination against women running, or women's personal or social situations? How much weight would you give to socialization?

3. Define gender role in your own words.

4. What roles do women play in politics now? (Think carefully. Political participation can range from supporting a particular party to holding an elected municipal, provincial or federal office.)

5. How do the roles you cited in (4) tie in with the gender roles for which women were socialized?

6. What is involved in adult socialization, and in resocialization?

7. The Hamilton Status of Women Committee wants more women to run for political office. What exactly are they trying to change to achieve this?

8. Does the way men are socialized mean that they are likely to support or resist women running for office?

9. How does a newspaper article like this play a role in resocializing men and women?

FIND A CLIPPING

Many newspaper comic strips include children. Look at these and select one that shows the child in interaction with an adult. Explain your interpretation of how the child, or adult, is being socialized in the encounter. Why is the cartoon funny?

8

Gender Roles

Gender refers to social, cultural and psychological characteristics of masculinity and femininity that are acquired by socialization. The appropriate norms governing behaviour for men and for women are learned in the process of socialization and reinforced in day-to-day relationships. Gender can therefore be understood as a socio-cultural elaboration of the differences between the sexes. Gender role refers to culturally defined attitudes and the behaviours that are widely accepted as appropriate for men and for women.

Gender is one basis of stratification. Most positions of power and prestige and control over property are held by men. Women for the most part do not have access to these resources. Most of the challenges to established gender roles are related to the differential life chances, power and prestige associated with gender.

Socially defined and established gender roles have also been challenged by both males and females as unnecessarily restrictive. It is argued that choices should be open to each person based on his or her personality, situation and needs, and not constrained by considerations of what is appropriate or allowed by gender. The

shift in thinking has been stimulated by several social factors, primarily the women's movement but also the changing economy, which has altered work and career patterns, and more recently, the male rebellion against their own prescribed roles.

As the traditional beliefs about the appropriate roles for women were widely challenged, this in turn significantly affected men's roles. Why, for example, should fathers not stay home to care for their young children, and mothers go out to work? Why are certain jobs regarded as female occupations, while others are considered exclusively male? Why are men not employed more frequently in day care, and as nurses? And why are so few women on the boards of corporations?

Gender roles permeate our thinking. Much tension has been created because the social expectations relating to male and female roles are now less clearly defined than in the recent past. It is very unsettling to accept any fundamental change in this area. The following two articles illustrate some of the problems and the need to examine our thinking about the roles played by men and women.

Impact on Individuals of Changing Social Roles

INTRODUCTION

This article deals with the psychological impact of social change on the male adult population. The psychologist claims that men are now in a more significant state of transition than women. A number of factors are related to this, two being cited in the article.

As you read this brief report, consider how people come to their perceptions of the world and of their place within it. Social change, and the psychological confusion that often follows, reveals the extent to which socially defined roles guide individuals' daily lives.

Men losing sense of purpose, psychologist says

By Wallace Immen

As women have more clearly defined their goals and desires, "men have lost their sense of purpose," says Herbert Freudenberger, the psychologist who coined the term burnout.

"American men are in a much more significant state of transition now than women," Dr. Freudenberger said yesterday during the annual meeting of the American Psychological Association in Toronto. "They are often uncertain, ambivalent about themselves and sometimes quite confused about the meaning of masculinity and what it means to act and 'be a man' in 1984."

It is only in the past few years that large numbers of men have sought psychological therapy, said Dr. Freudenberger, author of two books on success and anxiety.

Most of the male patients in his New York practice are between the ages of 25 and 50. While they are often successful in business, they feel depressed, insecure about the future and trapped in traditional family relationships.

The problem has arisen from changes in the traditional roles of women, Dr. Freudenberger said. Women are gaining power and control of themselves and are no longer dependent. "The bottom line is that men and women are in daily contact with each other," but large numbers of men are unable to adjust to the needs of women.

Men who cannot cope with the new order display a variety of symptoms:

- Many patients seem able to express their feelings verbally but their ability to be intimate in relationships is limited. "They know the rap but they don't know what it means." They may stay in a relationship for a while but then drift on to another. They say they feel trapped by relationships and often have few friends.
- They may become narcissistic and compulsive about an activity. Many become fanatics about a sport or running or the way they look.
- Others become addicted to chemicals such as alcohol, marijuana or cocaine. Dr. Freudenberger said he considers cocaine use the most unfortunate trend he has seen in the past few years. "It is incredibly difficult to get patients off it."
- Some men just drop out of their supportive role, preferring to manipulate a woman so she will nurture him.
- Many become impotent sexually.

One form of traditional escape, submerging yourself in your

work, no longer works for these men. Because of changes in technology and rapid acquisition of companies, men can no longer count on lifelong careers, Dr. Freudenberger said. "The world is no longer consistent and work doesn't act as gratification."

Both men and women will need to change their ideas to cope with modern society, "but the biggest change needs to be made by the men," Dr. Freudenberger said. "It will not be an easy task."

Men will also have to stop imposing their idea of reality on women and will have to take women's perspectives into account, he said.

Men will also have to learn how to measure their achievement in new terms—"Not just work but also achievement as a lover, mate, parent and friend."

Women, for their part, should be careful not to copy male models in the work world, he added. Instead of bringing humanism into the work world, many women are pushing themselves into the same health problems that plague men: alcoholism, heart disease and stress.

The Globe and Mail, Toronto, Saturday, August 25, 1984, pp. 1, 2.

Concepts to consider:

Economy, family, gender role, power, prestige, psychology, social change, social psychology, stress.

QUESTIONS

1. Explain the differences between psychology, social psychology, and sociology. Can sociologists use the findings of psychologists?

2. Define gender role.

3. What does it mean to be masculine in contemporary Canadian society? Is it a social definition you are trying to write, or a personal one? What is the difference? Is the social definition currently unclear?

4. Are people really so "hung up" on roles that when these roles change people "fall apart"? Discuss.

5. According to the article, what aspect of society is changing that is radically affecting men's lives?

6. What are "the needs of women" to which large numbers of men are unable to adjust, according to Dr. Freudenberger? Why should the adjustment be difficult?

7. How do men impose their idea of reality on women? How might women's perspectives differ?

8. Why is it that men find work stressful? Why should women find it the same? Is the stress level likely to increase?

9. Why should women bring humanism into the workplace? Is this part of the feminine role? Aren't men regarded as humanistic?

10. Briefly, how do functionalists, conflict theorists and social interactionists view the connections between men's roles and women's roles?

Real women do stay single

Examining the Social Pressure to Marry

INTRODUCTION

Marriage is institutionalized in our society. Most people do marry at least once in their lifetime and have children. In this article, Judith Timson gives her perception of the social pressures on those who do not marry.

Before you read the article, reflect on your own attitudes as well as those of other people you know regarding being single or being married. Consider how these attitudes apply to both males and females, and to peoples of various age groups. Where does the pressure to marry and raise a family come from? How fast are attitudes toward marriage changing?

By Judith Timson

On the occasion of her 50th birthday, feminist author and activist Gloria Steinem was interviewed by a reporter from The Washington Post named Molly Sinclair. The interview was widely circulated in North American newspapers. From the tone of her questioning, I imagined the interviewer to be woman wearing jackboots and a T-shirt emblazoned with the slogan: Real Women Don't Stay Single. To put it mildly, Molly was not nice to Gloria, although her opening question was fair enough: "You've never married. How do you feel about the prospect of growing old without children of your own and without being married?"

Gloria said she felt "terrific" about all this, but a few questions later, Molly was back at her: "You've never married, had children and you don't look like you have aged much. Where do you get off preaching about the importance of marriage and children and the plight of the older woman?" This time, Gloria explained that she had been able to experience some of these milestones secondhand by looking at the effect they had on other women. "The inequity of marriage made me not get married," was how she put it. But Molly, still dissatisfied, remained riveted on the central fact of Gloria's

singlehood: "Never in the whole 50 years did you meet somebody that you felt it would be worthwhile to negotiate some of those things?" Gloria held her ground, but Molly was having none of it. No, by her next question, she made it clear she thought poor Gloria had Ms'ed the boat: "Don't you feel even the slightest bit of envy for women (who have) children?"

The interview was depressing, partly because of the relentlessly negative approach it took to Gloria's life as a single woman but particularly because these feelings were coming from another woman. They were the kinds of questions that, if they had been asked by a man, a woman would recognize she was dealing with the "Why aren't you married, is there something wrong with you?" school of noncontemporary thinking and react accordingly.

But the fact that a woman was asking them indicates that society—including women—has not moved very far from the position that to be single is aberrant in a very major way; and for a woman over the age 35, it is still tantamount to being a sin, something for which she can be either vilified or pitied.

It was not so long ago in the popular culture that the single woman was glorified. Jill Clayburgh lolled around in her underpants and T-shirt in the movie *An Unmarried Woman,* rejecting Alan Bates in favor of self-discovery. Diane Keaton was neurotic but adorable as the single Annie Hall, although come to think of it she did get her skull bashed in while *Looking For Mr. Goodbar.* Today, very few movies feature the single woman as heroine. The '80s have become the age of commitment, or so we keep reading, and the singles scene, with the threat of herpes and the dreaded "man shortage," has become a nightmare, or so we are told by earnest T.V. documentaries.

In real life, however, single women bravely march on. Some of them have yet to find a person with whom they wish to spend their lives, others are divorced, still others widowed and some are secretly gay. Yet, most of them, at one point or another, have felt called upon to explain their lives or to correct their single status. I am not talking here about women who are very young. Most women who are single and in their 20s are not looked upon as aberrant, except perhaps by their mothers. It is when they move into their 30s that the word "still" is slipped pointedly in front of "single," and by their 40s, it is all over: they have become the women who "never married."

Why do we keep doing this to women? A man I know tells me that being single after a certain age is equally hard on men, but I don't believe him. I've heard of men chuckling over the fact that their families are trying to marry them off but I seldom hear a man describe the problem of being single in terms of significantly lowered self-esteem. I've never had a man tell me that he is afraid to go home to a family reunion because he is still single.

The source of this pressure on women is twofold. To marry is to legitimize yourself in the eyes of society, and most women I know who do marry will confess privately, if not publicly, that they felt relief at having done so. Not only had they taken themselves off the singles market, they had jumped through one of society's major hoops, acquiring respectability and added value at a single bound.

The second source is internal and a lot more complicated. All of the work being done recently in the field of women's psychology suggests that, for most women—whether they are working or not, high-powered or unambitious—emotional attachments are still what matter most in their lives. It is in terms of these attachments that a woman measures her worth. While very few people—male or female—want to drift through life without a strong sexual and emo-

tional bond with someone else (which usually means marriage or, at the very least, a long-term, established domestic partnership), for women to do without this bond creates an unhappy cycle of desperation and depression.

A woman whose domestic responsibilities include the teen-age daughter of the man she lives with reports that the young woman and her friends seem to have a refreshing "take it or leave it" attitude toward men. If the men, or boys, they are seeing fit in with their plans, that's great. If they don't, too bad for them. It will be interesting to see if they have the same amount of sang froid in their 30s.

In the meantime, we take one step forward and two steps back (hello, Molly).

When I got married last summer at the age of 32, my status on the marriage licence read "never married." The clerk at Toronto City Hall, where we had gone to pick up the licence, proudly told me I was lucky: "A couple of years ago, the word would have been 'spinster,' but we're not allowed to use that anymore." I suppose it is a good sign that they've taken the word "spinster" out of our officially approved vocabulary. It will take just a little bit longer to get it out of our minds.

Chatelaine, August 1984, p. 36.

Concepts to consider:

Esteem, role, gender role, marriage, prestige, romantic love, social institution, socialization, values, symbol.

QUESTIONS

1. Define gender roles. Is getting married part of the role.

2. Identify the key points of the author's argument.

3. Do you think Judith Timson is wrong in her perceptions that single women are viewed negatively?

4. What theoretical perspective would you use to explain the negative attitude towards single women?

5. Does a single woman's social prestige vary depending on whether she has never married, is living with a man, been divorced, or widowed, or is gay? Can you explain, in sociological terms, why this should be so?

6. Have you ever personally experienced pressure to get married? If so, compare your experience with someone of the opposite sex. Have they experienced pressure to get married? What are the similarities and the differences compared to your experience?

7. "Spinster"... what are the connotations of this word? Why is it negative?

8. This article comes from <u>Chatelaine</u>, a popular magazine designed for women. Presumably the editors think that issues relating to relations between the sexes are of interest to women. Is it an issue of interest to men too? Explain why or why not.

FIND A CLIPPING

Many occupations are considered male occupations, others are almost exclusively female. Hiring practices are changing, and the sex stereotyping of occupations is changing slowly, but the distinction persists in many types of work.

Find a clipping that describes a job that is almost always done by a man, or by a woman. Explain why this situation persists. What are the difficulties of hiring someone of the opposite sex to perform the same work?

9

Aging

We are all aging, and we live in an age-graded society. Age in years simply marks the passage of time. But associated with age are certain culturally defined stages of life. Being "elderly" or a "senior citizen" is an ascribed status, as is being a teenager or middle aged. Individuals do not choose the status, but it affects their self-image and others' image of them. The image may be positive or negative, depending on the circumstances. A man job-hunting who is in late middle age may find his age viewed negatively by prospective employers, and his self-image suffers. Middle-aged women, their child-raising duties completed, may feel they are too old to start on a career of paid work.

The age composition of the population affects the social structure (or social organization). For example, as more people live longer, and stay healthy, there may be changes in the area of work; compulsory retirement has already been challenged in many jobs as discriminatory, allowing some employees to continue working. As the population of older people increases, the services offered by the private sector of the economy will increase. The first article in this section, on housing, is an example of this trend. The economic welfare of the over-65 population will become an issue as providing pensions for greater numbers becomes expensive. Also, as their numbers grow proportionately faster than the rest of the population, older citizens are gaining increasing political influence.

The older population should never be thought of as a homogeneous group. For starters, think of the age span covered by the term "senior citizen": there is a great difference between 65 or 85 years old. (Compare it with being 18, or 38.)

There are also enormous variations in income and health status. In the higher age brackets, women greatly outnumber men. All these variables have important implications for the individual's private family life, relations with others, and the use and provision of social and medical services.

The second article in this section advertises social activities for seniors. The "appropriate" activities and responsibilities for older citizens is to a large extent prescribed and proscribed by cultural definitions. Older people who want to do something different from what is the norm for their age are variously described as difficult, stubborn, independent, wonderful, senile, eccentric, "great for their age," "quite a character," remarkable and so on. In fact, there is likely to be more individuality in activities in the higher age brackets because of the variety of interests related to past experiences and opportunities. Energy level and state of health also influence older people's participation, as they do for all age levels.

Many images and connotations are conveyed by the terms used to describe the over-50 population: senior citizen, veteran, pensioner, old-age pensioner, elderly, old, aged, middle aged, late middle aged, past middle age, oldster, senior, "getting on in years," centenarian, "past it," "over the hill," "out to pasture," "old fogey." Consider the symbolism in the labels applied to the older population and the impact they have on people's perception of themselves and others.

Aging affects the organization of the society as well as individuals' self image, and their definition of their situation within the social structure.

Age Segregated Housing

INTRODUCTION

Housing in Canada is provided both by government and by private developers, and is either rented or sold. The type of housing a family occupies is commonly seen as an indicator of their social class.

Cities and towns develop over time, and this history often leads to some areas in the city having a higher percentage of older people than other areas that attract young families. Age differentiation can thus occur "naturally" in response to economic and social influences over time. In the case of Horizon Village and other similar developments, a housing area is created that deliberately excludes young people. The age limitation is imposed by the developers of the project who wish to appeal to potential buyers. Life within this housing complex will be significantly influenced both by the age of the residents, the type of housing, and the particular category of over-50-year-olds attracted to it.

T.V. Times, The Edmonton Journal, May 4 to 11, 1984, p. 23. With permission of Horizon Retirement Corporation.

Concepts
to consider:

**Age grade, category,
demography, economy,
ideology, social class, social
interaction, status, symbol.**

QUESTIONS

1. Horizon Village is in St. Albert, an upper-middle-class community on the outskirts of Edmonton. In sociological terms, explain exactly why the equivalent accommodation would not be available in a low-income inner-city area. Or is it?

2. What categories of people will move into Horizon Village?

3. What services does the management of Horizon Village offer to residents? Why is it thought these would appeal to this age group?

4. What are people avoiding by choosing to live in Horizon Village? Think carefully! Go beyond the advertisement.

5. How would age-segregated housing affect social interaction between the residents and others both inside and outside Horizon Village?

6. How would living in this kind of housing affect the residents' world view?

7. What is the symbolism in the name of the development? Is this likely to sell the housing?

8. How have the potential occupants "earned it"? Is this the truth or a rationalization?

Social Interaction in Old Age

INTRODUCTION

A large proportion of people's lives is spent in association with others. From these contacts they gain an understanding of themselves, a sense of identity, and a feeling of having a place in society. When people of any age become isolated they lose this sense of identity and their feeling of place. This happens to older people if they cannot, or choose not to, substitute new group contacts to replace the ones they have lost through retirement or because of their inability to continue activities. Most people need to find friendship and support to enable them to adjust to life changes. For older people this may be more difficult to do if they lack the physical energy to seek out new contacts. For some, social and support needs can be met by joining organizations where other members have had similar adjustment problems.

Many of the organizations catering to senior citizens have been started and are run by younger people. Their definition of what are appropriate activities for older people may decide what is programmed unless the participants are allowed considerable input.

Keep Active

By Shirley Dereniski

Loneliness, depression and anxiety are common at all ages. The post-retirement years may bring additional stress such as leaving the labor force, illness, or the loss of friends and family. Participation in active leisure pursuits provides renewed opportunities for fun and social involvement. In addition, studies have shown moderately vigorous activity to be more effective than the use of tranquilizers in the release of tension, anger or frustration.

Active individuals sleep better and relax more readily. In addition, sports and exercise can help reduce physical and psychological tension. Hobbies and handicrafts provide an outlet for creative expression while helping to maintain fine motor skills and muscle functioning in the hands and fingers.

The Senior Adult Development Committee has undertaken several programs to assist seniors in Yorkton.

The Senior Olympics Committee held its first meeting Monday, June 4. Plans are underway for this special sports event for seniors in Yorkton and area. Some of the events to be included will be slow pitch, shuffleboard, horseshoe pitch, carpet bowling, darts, pool and cribbage. Anyone interested in working with this committee is invited to call.

Job Bureau

A Job Bureau has now been established. If you are a senior and are in need of help with simple repairs in and around your home, there may be someone to help you out. We have a number of experienced seniors willing to help other seniors for a small fee.

Socials

A social evening for widowed seniors has been planned for June 12, 7 p.m., at SIGN, 29 Livingstone Street. It is hoped this will become a monthly event to help newly widowed persons adjust to their situation. This is your invitation to attend. Come and bring a friend.

Yorkton Enterprise, Saskatchewan, Wednesday, June 6, 1984, p. 12A. Information taken from "Don't Take it Easy" by Government of Canada, Department of Fitness and Amateur Sport.

Concepts to consider:

Age grade, category, formal organization, group, network, norms, peer group, social class, social interaction.

QUESTIONS

1. Growing old was described by one older person as "the greatest adventure of his lifetime." Do you think that growing old is an exciting adventure? Why or why not? Do social attitudes influence you?

2. Which age group is the target audience for this article and for the activities it advertises?

3. Are the kind of activities considered suitable for seniors socially defined?

4. Look at the problems listed in the first paragraph. In your opinion would "participation in leisure activities" help to mitigate the problems?

5. Do seniors need organized groups for support and social contact? Explain why.

6. How should the groups be organized? Consider how the way in which the group is organized will affect its functioning.

7. Review the article. Do you find the general tone positive or negative? If you were a senior citizen, is there anything about this article that you would find demeaning or patronizing? Consider both words and content.

8. Does society sideline senior citizens, or do senior citizens sideline themselves?

9. Does social class have an impact on the groups and activities in which senior citizens participate?

FIND A CLIPPING

As senior citizens become more numerous in Canadian society they will collectively have more political influence. Politicians will pay attention to the interests of the elderly in federal, provincial or in civic elections. Older people are now forming interest groups and lobbying for particular services or changes that they desire.

Find a clipping that reflects the political clout of a section of the older population. Describe exactly what the issue is, and how the interests of this age group are being addressed. Include in your discussion the sociological context within which the action takes place.

10

Population

Demography is the scientific study of human populations. The three factors that collectively determine the size of the population are births, deaths and migration. Sociologists are interested in the relationship between social factors and population changes. There is an interaction between birth rates, death rates and migration rates, and the social and economic life of the country. Cultural values and religious beliefs relating to family life, for example, will affect decisions about family size, and smaller families in turn are a contributing factor in the increasing number of women working outside the home. In times of high unemployment and economic recession the birth rate will drop, reflecting potential parents' fears of difficulties in supporting children and concern for their future.

The life span of both men and women has increased steadily over past decades, reflecting improvements in housing, sanitation, and food as well as improved medical care. Those areas of the country that still have poor access to medical care have a higher death rate, especially in infant mortality, which has a long-term impact on population increase.

Push-pull factors affect migration. Push factors refer to unfavourable conditions that encourage people to move out. Pull factors are those positive influences that persuade people to settle in a particular area. For example, countries, or regions within the country, and communities with a high standard of living will attract immigrants, while those areas with a low standard of living will lose their mobile individuals. Thus, internal migra-

tion within Canada reflects the economic conditions in different regions: boom areas experience an influx of job seekers, which has an impact on the age structure of the population in that area since those who move tend to be young adults, who then settle and raise their families in the new community.

Thus migration, as well as natural increase, affects the size and distribution of the population within a country such as Canada, and this in turn affects the distribution of economic and political power. The more populated areas are commonly those of greatest economic activity and, in a democratic society, these populated areas also have the greatest political influence.

Population size is also affected by government policy on immigration. Canada has always been regarded as a land of immigrants, but in times of economic recession the number of immigrants allowed to enter Canada is restricted. Since most immigrants are young, this has a double impact in terms of number of immigrants, and their potential contribution to the birth rate. A restrictive immigration policy, combined with a low birth rate among Canadians, will lead to an aging population. This issue is examined in the first article in this section.

The second article deals with the interpretation and use of population statistics, using Newfoundland as an example. The third article illustrates the way in which entrepreneurs in a free enterprise economy use population statistics to judge which segment of the population is a profitable market.

Determinants of Canada's Future Population

INTRODUCTION

Population size, age structure and growth rates are determined by births, deaths, and net migration. This article draws on a report put out by Statistics Canada, Fertility in Canada: From Baby-Boom to Baby-Bust. Population forecasts are based on statistical projections using well established methodology. The harder things to predict are the social factors that will influence birth rates, immigration and emigration, and death rates.

The theory of demographic transition was deduced from the study of population statistics in western European societies. The theory takes into account changes in the social and economic life of the society. For example, couples choose to have fewer children in a society where children represent an economic burden rather than an economic asset and when infant mortality has declined, so that more children survive.

As you read the article, focus on the interaction between social, cultural, and economic trends and changes and population.

Baby-boom fertility rates plummeting

By Dorothy Lipovenko

Canada will need 275,000 immigrants by the year 2000 to keep the population growing because the baby-boom generation has sent fertility rates plummeting to their lowest since the Depression, a Statistics Canada report says.

If the present fertility rate of 1.7 births per woman persists or drops, it will result in a "dramatic shift" in the age structure of Canada's population, warns the report, Fertility in Canada: From Baby-Boom to Baby-Bust, released yesterday.

Fewer young people will be available to care for an increasingly elderly population of baby-boomers reaching retirement. Ultimately they will account for 25 per cent of the population. In 1981, only 10 per cent of the population was over 65.

The report by demographer Anatole Romaniuc warns Canadians to start planning now for the massive impact on old age services, pensions and health care plans when the baby-boom generation reaches retirement in the 2020s.

The report provides the first statistical evidence that baby-boomers, the generation born in the 15 or so years following the Second World War and now in their child-bearing prime, are responsible for Canada's baby-bust – a trend which is common internationally.

"If the fertility rate does not increase substantially and if population growth is a national goal, then large-scale immigration is clearly the alternative," the report says. The trend to fewer babies and a growing old population "are creating a historically new situation, which may affect long-term immigration strategies."

Employment and Immigration Minister Flora MacDonald said recently that Canada's slowing population growth will be a major factor in determining immigration levels.

The Statscan report warns that Canada's fertility rate of 1.7 births per woman – is "well below the replacement level" of 2.1 children and below the Depression's fertility rate of 2.6 births per woman. Near the end of the baby boom in 1959, women averaged 3.9 births.

The report blames many sociological factors for the low reproductive rates, notably the changing role of women, particularly their influx into the paid work force, the decision of many men and women to marry later or not at all and, among married couples delayed child-bearing or a deliberate choice to remain childless.

The rising divorce rate and greater availability of contraception and abortion are also blamed for the recent trend to smaller families.

Quebec has one of the lowest provincial fertility rates – 1.5 births per woman – and even Canada's native people, who had large families until the mid-1960s, dropped from 7 to 3.5 births per woman by the late seventies.

In Quebec, it is estimated that half of the women who were 40 years old in 1980 had undergone sterilization of one type or another. Sterilization has become the most popular method of birth control among older couples in Quebec and is increasingly being used by younger couples still in their early child-rearing years, the report said.

In an interview, Dr. Romaniuc predicted Canada will need to admit 500,000 immigrants annually by the year 2050 to sustain population growth at a moderate 1 per cent. But the low fertility rate may be reversed by the children born to baby-boomers, Dr. Romaniuc said, because "they will grow up in a less competitive environment and may want to marry earlier."

Canada's low fertility rate does not mean an imminent decline in the population, he said. Even in the absence of any immigration, Canada's population will grow slowly and should reach 26.5 million by the turn of the century, because there will be enough women of child-bearing age "to more than compensate" for individual women who are not having more than two children.

A small boost to the population is happening now as working women who delayed child-bearing race to meet a biological deadline. Almost 25 per cent of babies born in 1982 to women over 30 were first-born children, making this the highest rate of older new parents Canada has ever had, the report said.

The report also confirms that Canada's age structure is chang-

Concepts to consider:

Birth rate, culture, death rate, demographic transition, economy, emigration, fertility rate, government, immigration, net migration, population size, religion, values.

ing rapidly. The number of people over 65 has almost doubled in 20 years to 2.3 million in 1981. Its rate of increase is twice that of the population as a whole.

The document called on the federal and provincial governments to formulate new social policies that will provide women with institutional support, such as improved day care, to ease the stress from the dual pressure of being a parent and working outside the home.

"As an alternative to fertility, immigration in numbers far in excess of the historical levels required to maintain even a moderate population growth, may be unattainable or attainable at considerable social cost. Public opinion could then eventually tip in favor of a more pro-natalist stance," the Statscan report said.

The Globe and Mail, Toronto, Thursday, December 20, 1984, pp. 1,2.

QUESTIONS

1. Why is the generation born from 1947 to the early 1960s called the "baby boom" generation?

2. Define birth rate. List all the influences you can think of that might explain the low birth rates cited in the article.

3. Explain what is meant by the fertility rate. How does the fertility rate affect the age structure?

4. Why is it considered desirable to maintain population growth? Think about the reasons given or implied in the article. What other reasons can you think of?

5. Why does Statistics Canada predict that Canada will need 270,000 immigrants by the year 2000? Explain carefully.

6. How precisely can the government influence immigration levels? Give both the direct and the indirect means.

7. What barriers are there to a significant increase in immigration?

8. Besides day care, what other "institutional supports" would encourage women to have more children?

9. Briefly outline the theory of demographic transition. What stage is Canada at now?

Interpreting and Using Vital Statistics

INTRODUCTION

In all provinces it is a legal requirement that all births, deaths and marriages be registered. The statistics are compiled and used for a wide variety of purposes from planning social services to calculating provincial equalization payments, and from calculating the future need for schools to providing entrepreneurs with figures on potential markets.

To use the figures constructively, they must be understood and interpreted correctly. This newspaper report is probably not very useful to the majority of readers; nevertheless, many municipal officials, civil servants, business people, voluntary agencies, medical services and school boards will find the data informative and will follow up on it in planning future programmes.

July top month for weddings during 1982

June may be the traditional month for weddings, but not in Newfoundland—at least during 1982.

July was the month when the most wedding bells rang throughout the province, with the Vital Statistics Division of the Department of Health recording 698 betrothals.

August was number two on the list of popular months, with 596 weddings and June third, with 383 marriages.

In 1982, there was a total of 3,764 marriages in the province, says the 1982 report on births, marriages and deaths, which was released Thursday.

The number of marriages in the province reached a peak of 5,106 in 1972 and dropped to 3,758 in 1981.

In 1982, 3,202 of the marriages were between people who had never been married before. Of the total number of marriages, 89 per cent included men who had never been married before and 91 per cent women who had never been married before.

Of the men who got married in 1982, 243 were under 20; of the women, 761 were under 20.

There were 9,173 births in the province in 1982, up from 9,120 in 1981 – a long way from the highest number of births recorded, 15,591 in 1961.

Of the 9,173 births, 4,642 were boys and 4,531 girls.

The busiest month in the province's maternity wards was March, with 851 births; there were 829 in September and 817 in July.

Illegitimate births increased, to 1,799 in 1982 from 1,730 in 1981.

The Vital Statistics Division estimates the province's population at the end of 1982, at 569,200. The Avalon Peninsula is estimated to have the highest population, with 241,200 people.

The number of deaths in the province rose to 3,385 in 1982 from 1981; of the 1982 total, 1,980 were men and 1,405 women.

Heart disease was the biggest killer, claiming 1,237 lives, an increase of 127 from 1981. Cancer claimed 763 lives, 48 more than in 1981.

The number of accidental deaths dropped to 244 in 1982 from 266 in 1981. Motor vehicles were the single largest cause of accidental deaths, claiming 66 men's lives and 14 women's lives.

The evening Telegram, St. John's, Friday, November 9, 1984, p. 4.

Concepts to consider:

Birth rate, culture, death rate, demography, marriage, migration, statistics, values.

QUESTIONS

1. Why do provinces keep records of births, deaths and marriages? Think as widely as possible for all the possible uses of this information.

2. Why are certain months favoured for weddings? What use is this information and to whom?

3. There are a number of possible reasons why the number of marriages in Newfoundland has dropped from the peak in 1972. Give as many reasons as you can think of.

4. What action might be taken, and by whom, to reverse this trend?

5. Why might the number of births have dropped from 1973 to 1983?

6. Why are illegitimate births singled out for separate mention? Explain the values behind why this statistic is kept.

7. Can you calculate the crude death rate from the figures given in the article?

8. Why is the number of deaths going up? Is it a significant rise?

9. The cause of death is always recorded. What use might this information be, and to whom?

10. From the figures given in the article, is it possible to make any predictions about the size of the Newfoundland population? What else would you need to know?

Demographic Changes and Economic Opportunities

INTRODUCTION

An aging population has an impact on the economy, and on the production, distribution and consumption of goods and services.

In a free enterprise system business people try to market goods to the largest number of consumers to maximize profits. They have to keep an eye on the market for their product and for opportunities to sell new products. Over time the consumer market may undergo demographic changes to which entrepreneurs must respond if they are not to "lose out." This article from The Financial Post explores the changes taking place and the opportunities in marketing to the older segment of the Canadian population.

Taking aim at the 'wellderly'

By Frances Phillips

We live in a culture that puts a premium on youth and youthfulness, but age we will, and manufacturers of many goods and services are gearing up for a mini-boom in the seniors market.

While overall population growth is slowing, the seniors market is expanding, and this trend is projected to accelerate as we move toward the year 2000.

Between 1970 and 1990 it is estimated Canada's total population will increase by 28 per cent, while the plus-60 segment is expected to grow by 47 per cent. In 1990, one out of every five adult Canadians will be over 60 years of age.

Opportunity knocks for marketers in over-the-counter pharmaceuticals, health aids, and nutrition-improved foods, in travel, investment funds, and home repair services.

The banks have been particularly aggressive in tapping into the mature market, with special savings and checking privileges for account holders. Some even make "house calls" to senior citizen residences.

Marketing opportunities take on broader proportions within the 45 – 59 age group, especially when measured against the under-30s segment.

The 45 – 59 group is projected to increase 54 per cent in the 1981 – 2001 period. On the other hand, statistics show the under-30s segment—the darling of many marketers these days—*declining* by 6% in the same period. Even today, advertisers targeting messages to the 18 – 49 group are missing one-third of the adult Canadian market.

Marketing and research house A.C. Nielsen dubs the mature market the "wellderly."

With children living away from home and mortgage payments out of the way, many upper and middle-class Canadians find themselves relatively well off in their senior years. As a rule, they are more active, more educated, and more conscious of their looks than their parents were. In the cosmetics industry, for instance, it is estimated 25 per cent of all sales are to the plus-60 age group.

And the wellderly have time to spare for quieter occupations, like reading. So it is no accident that three publications targeting the graying generation make their debut this month.

With the addition of Prime, a bi-monthly magazine from Montreal publisher Douglas Squarek and Maturity magazine in Surrey, B.C., Canadians now have three publications serving this market.

The Elder Statesman, another magazine sold in British Columbia, is under new management and has just published a 64-page Handbook for Seniors, which will be distributed free at branches of the Bank of British Columbia and

Shoppers Drug Mart stores in the province.

"We are certainly taking the market seriously," says Gerald Kidd, 51, publisher of The Elder Statesman.

Maturity, a controlled circulation magazine making its debut this month, is available at 90 Pharmasave stores and 158 Bank of Montreal branches in B.C.

The latest entry to hit the streets is Prime, and the 20,000 copies supplied to newsstands this month are reported to have sold briskly at $2.25 a copy.

Up-beat

Billed as "the only national magazine for contemporary people over 40," the digest-size magazine kicked off its premier issue with profiles of Global TV's Jan Tennant (47) and dancer John Stanzel (61). The tempo is up-beat and positive. Indeed, the only concession to its target audience is a slightly larger type face for easy reading.

Squarek says we are beginning to see a reluctant awareness and acceptance of aging. He is encouraged by the "sprinkling of intelligent advertising" now appearing in the media, which doesn't picture older men and women as stooped and infirm and relegated to feeding the pigeons from a park bench.

Publications targeting the mature market are not new. Several have made guest appearances over the years, only to find they were a little before their time.

In the U.S., however, Modern Maturity has become the third-largest magazine in that country (after Readers Digest and National Geographic), with a circulation base of 9.2 million. Circulation is expected to climb a further 1.3 million by next year.

Leonard Kubas, of Kubas Research Consultants, Toronto, says that "marketing for older people may not be as terrific as first meets the eye." These consumers are pretty well settled in terms of their physical needs, he says, and many people 50 years old and over eke out a modest life.

"Mature consumers are more experienced consumers, and when they see a new ad for a Chevrolet, they are not necessarily convinced that they should be driving a Chevy," says Kubas.

StatCan estimates that 56 per cent of Canadians over 65 years of age who did not live with relatives or in institutional settings in 1982 spent at least 58 per cent of their income on necessities like food, shelter and clothing—leaving them little to play with in terms of disposable income.

But with an eye to the future, most marketers are monitoring today's 50-year-olds. The majority live in their own homes, which are close to being paid for (although some 20 per cent do rent), and for the most part, this group has quite different values than did the previous generation. Its members tend to be more confident in their decision-making abilities, they are more open-minded about trying new products, and they are more politicized.

A conference held by the Canadian Council of Better Business Bureaus recently served as a primer to marketers on the mature market and the opportunities that exist there.

General Mills Canada Ltd. in Toronto is looking at this market already. It is redesigning labels to highlight the ingredients list with a larger typeface, and food scientists in the company laboratory are reformulating products to provide greater nutritional benefits to users of all ages.

But there still exist many untapped opportunities in fashion, computers and leisure activities.

Seniors should not be perceived as caricatures of "little old ladies," said Doug Rapelje, director of the Senior Citizens department for the regional municipality of Niagara, Ont., at the BBB conference. While chronologically old, mature folk don't necessarily feel their age. They want to dress, drive, travel and enjoy life just as they did when they were young.

The Financial Post, September 22, 1984, p. 11. With permission of The Financial Post.

Concepts to consider:

Age structure, consumption, culture, distribution, economy, ideology, mass media, production, stereotype, values.

QUESTIONS

1. Explain what the writer means by the "wellderly". Why is there now a significant number of people who can be so labelled?

2. Why do they capture the interest of advertisers and entrepreneurs?

3. How do the consumer interests of the wellderly differ from those in younger age brackets?

4. To what does "disposable income" refer?

5. What values are likely to guide older consumers in the spending of their disposable income? Do similar values guide younger (20 – 49 years) consumers?

6. What factors do publishers consider when starting a new magazine?

7. What makes people stereotype the old?

8. Will making the older age groups a valued market work against stereotyping?

9. From the point of view of manufacturers and of advertisers, what are the snags in marketing to an older age group?

FIND A CLIPPING

Migration is a response to both push factors and pull factors.

Find an article which deals with immigration to or emigration from Canada, or migration within Canada.

Identify the push factors and pull factors that are stimulating this migration. Use both information in the article and your own knowledge of the cultural, social, economic, political and geographic characteristics of the sending and receiving locales.

11

Ethnic Groups

Canada is a pluralistic society. Many ethnic groups try to maintain their distinctive ethnic culture while being part of the larger Canadian culture. The ethnic sub-culture may involve language, beliefs, values and norms that are different from, and perhaps in sharp contrast to, those of the dominant culture. Ethnic cultures which differ from the culture of the majority can be undermined by constant and daily competition in language, values and lifestyles experienced in the workplace, school, or social life, and portrayed in the mass media. To survive, an ethnic group's cultural heritage must not only be shared but must also be constantly reinforced through interaction with others from the same ethnic background. In addition, it must also be passed on to the next generation. Many ethnic groups fear that if they do not strive to preserve their heritage it will quickly be eroded. The native people of northern Canada, in particular, feel that their way of life will be lost if they do not take steps to preserve it. With increased economic activity in the North and the constant barrage of non-native cultural images via television and radio, their fears are probably well grounded.

Many immigrants who came to Canada are not concerned about maintaining their culture; they have assimilated into the majority culture and identify themselves as Canadian. Others maintain some of their distinctive ethnic customs, traditions and beliefs. Still others feel that their ethnic identity must be maintained intact even though they also identify themselves as Canadians. Many groups came to settle in Canada because of promises of freedom, after experiencing persecution in countries they left. Canadian multiculturalism encourages individuals to make a free choice on whether or not they wish to maintain their distinctive culture.

Canada has a great variety of different ethnic groups and an official policy of multiculturalism, yet prejudice and discrimination still exist. Some immigrants experience differential treatment based on their race, as do the native Indian and Metis people; the visible minorities, even if they choose to assimilate, are not always allowed to do so. Social life is competitive; people compete for social and economic rewards (wealth, positions giving a high income, power and prestige). Being distinctive, either racially or culturally, can lead to being treated in a discriminatory way and being denied access to these social rewards.

The concepts of minority group and majority group focus on the power that each group can command—not on numbers. The majority group is the dominant group in the society, not necessarily the most numerous. Not all minority groups are ethnic groups: women, the handicapped, homosexuals, and the aged are also examples of minority groups. Minority groups have distinctive ascribed characteristics, and experience discrimination on the basis of them. Minority-group status has an impact on an individual's self-image, and group members may develop a sense of collective identity as a result.

The two articles that follow explore these issues further.

Ways in Which Ethnic Identity Can Be Eroded or Preserved

INTRODUCTION

Many factors influence the preservation, or loss, of ethnic identity. The mass media are but one factor, yet they are one that has a very pervasive influence.

The writer of this aritcle, David Porter, vice-chairman of the Council for Yukon Indians, expresses his concern over further potential intrusion into the northern people's culture through expanded radio and T.V. services provided by southern stations.

Radio and television can be used to the advantage of the native people by providing communications links over long distances in the north. If the native people were involved in production and programming, the cultural images they would see on the screen and hear on the air waves would be their own, not those of the white culture.

Porter is not against change or modernization. His concern is to avoid allowing modernization to erode native culture and sense of identity further. To understand his point of view, imagine the reverse—radio and television for southern Canada entirely created and produced by native people, offering news, documentaries, and entertainment from their cultural standpoint.

Give us a chance to be equals

By David Porter

Colonial governments. Pipelines, natural resource exploitation, racism, loss of rights, culture and land. Northern native peoples, the Inuit of the Arctic, Déné of the Mackenzie Valley and the Yukon Indians face relentless erosion of their aboriginal rights by a dominant society. We spend our lives defending our culture from the ravages of so-called progress. It's a mighty struggle, and more often than not we lose. But on this one occasion, we might just turn the tide. The Council for Yukon Indians (C.Y.I.) and the Déné Nation have jointly applied to the Canadian Radio-television and Telecommuncations Commission (C.R.T.C.) for a licence to operate a radio broadcasting network and to produce television programming in the Far North. It's the first step in a comprehensive communcations initiative leading, ultimately, to what we hope will be a television channel devoted exclusively to native programming.

In this historic collaboration, the C.Y.I. and Déné Nation represent all Indians, status and non-status, north of the 60th parallel. Our application calls for technology, facilities and programming that will originate in the North, as well as provide unprecedented communication from one northern community to another. We have applied for a graduated program of communications development. The first phase would involve a complete radio service, with native-language commentary, local control and community-to-community radio linkups. Every issue important to our people could be discussed through these radio conferences. What the South takes for granted, the North would finally obtain.

In the second phase, we hope to introduce several hours of original prime-time T.V. programming and, in the third phase, our own television channel. As things now stand, the CBC has indicated that it cannot provide the required services. Nor did the 11 commercial applicants who appeared before the C.R.T.C propose a plan sufficiently comprehensive to include such service. Yet it is surely obvious that any proposal that lacks northern origination— which lacks a specifically northern focus—is simply a proposal to extend further the domination of southern television over the North.

So at last month's C.R.T.C. hearings in Ottawa we sought additional guarantees. We demanded certain conditions of any commercial operators who would be bringing services to our communities. And the conditions are pretty explicit. They include our control over which programming and communications services will be brought into the North, guarantees of training courses for our people, some prime time on commercial channels devoted to native programming and some to the technical facilities to make it all possible. In other words, it will take partnership if the grandly ambitious scheme of servicing the North is to work. The role of ensuring that the individual communities will actually receive programs, any programs, can only be filled by the mutual cooperation of government, commercial applicants and the Council for Yukon Indians/Déné Nation.

Admittedly, the more than 40,000 northern native people in the Yukon and Northwest Territories represent only a small section of the population of six million or so that will benefit from the extension of service. But our people must be seen as a primary beneficiary—a communications infrastructure is critical to our social and economic development. Without the ability to receive radio and television programming, or to commmunicate among the communities themselves, entire areas remain isolated, discriminated against, underdeveloped and under-served.

But above all, such technological development can never succeed unless it is adapted to the culture and needs of the people to be served. Our people are at a crossroads. On one hand, we are the product of a rich and ancient culture. On the other, we are forcibly determined by modern society. The struggle is visceral; the direction taken is crucial.

The C.R.T.C. issued a challenge to native people to get involved and we answered that challenge. We want to learn and to develop with this new communications technology, but we must also safeguard our culture. There can be no sacrifice of one for the other. We know that it's an enormous jump to go from snowshoes to satellite communications. Chief Dan George said it well: "If you have travelled far, I have travelled further. To go from the age of bows and arrows to people walking on the moon is a very, very long way."

We have never said that we're not willing to make changes. We seek to make things better for our people, but the acceptance of modern ways shouldn't mean emasculating our identity. We are more than willing to welcome this new communications technology, and we will make a thoughtful contribution to its development. We're neither dogmatic nor inflexible, but the needs and strengths and wishes of our people must be central. In today's highly competitive world, no one can afford the penalties of silence—we need to build bridges of understanding.

So far we have survived by adapting to our surroundings, and we will continue to survive. In the past we applied our creativity and skills to surviving in the harsh North. We are masters of living by balancing the demand of our environment with our need to survive. But the core of this adaptation is to seek equality with the world around us.. We must not be denied this opportunity.

Maclean's, March 23, 1981, p. 8.

Concepts to consider:

Culture, ethnic group, majority group, minority group, power, sub-culture, technology.

QUESTIONS

1. Explain why the culture of an ethnic group distinguishes it from other groups within a society.

2. Can the Yukon Indians, the Déné, and the Inuit be called ethnic groups?

3. Explain the sociological meaning of minority group. Can northern native people be called a minority group?

4. Explain what is meant by majority group. How does the majority group affect the minority group or groups?

5. David Porter refers to "a proposal to extend further the domination of southern television over the North." Why are northern native leaders concerned about this?

6. Porter refers to a number of issues and developments that he sees as a "relentless erosion of... aboriginal rights by the dominant society" and as a threat to native culture. List them.

7. Take one of the factors you mentioned above and examine how it would damage native people's rights or culture.

8. Why would the Council for Yukon Indians and the Déné Nation want ot be involved in all aspects of developing radio and T.V. programming for the North?

9. Explain how the traditional culture and the new technology might be reconciled and the amalgam used to help native people preserve their identity. Use your own ideas.

Reverse Discrimination— Arguments For and Against

INTRODUCTION

Some ethnic groups are significantly under-represented in high-status occupational groups. Lack of access to positions providing high income, influence and power means that individuals cannot improve their personal position, nor can they provide role models for others of the same ethnic background.

Prejudice refers to attitudes that pre-judge persons on the basis of their group membership without regard to their individual characteristics. Discriminatory actions may follow from the prejudiced attitude. Employers' hiring practices or the criteria for hiring often discriminate against certain groups within Canadian society. Many ethnic groups are among those suffering from discriminatory hiring.

The establishment and enforcment of non-discriminary hiring practices would open up employment opportunities for visible minorities despite prejudicial attitudes and would reinforce those unprejudiced employers in their inclination to hire from all racial and ethnic groups. Prejudiced employers would be forced to re-examine their position. Reverse discrimination would enforce preferential treatment for specific racial groups. Consider it an option, but consider also the arguments that are made against it.

Racial quotas in job world may be remedy for Canada

By Arthur Schafer

(Mr. Schafer is a professor of philosophy at the University of Manitoba.)

"Discrimination is discrimination is discrimination." The central point of this refrain seems to be that discrimination, in any form, is always and everywhere morally wrong. To persuade Canadians that there are circumstances in which discrimination is good rather than evil will be no easy task.

When the House of Commons Special Committee on Visible Minorities in Canadian Society included among its 80 recommendations one favoring hiring and promotion quotas for racial minorites, its report met a storm of protest. The idea of racial quotas—even when intended to benefit disadvantaged minorites—touches a raw nerve in liberally minded Canadians. Predictably, reaction from the media has been almost uniformly hostile to any policy favoring reverse discrimination (preferential treatment for members of a group that has previously suffered discrimination), especially when this takes the form of quotas.

Now that the flurry of hostile reaction has subsided, it may be time to re-examine the arguments that surround the use of quotas to correct past injustices and current imbalances of opportunity, income and status in Canadian society.

Defenders of reverse discrimination must attempt to rebut the deeply held belief that discrimination is always wrong.

As an example, suppose that an international college is established (like the Lester B. Pearson College of the Pacific) with a major goal of exposing its students to the views and cultures of students from other nations. To promote this admirable concept, a quota system is used to achieve the proper international "mix". Some academically qualified applicants are bound to be refused admission because the quota for their geographical region has been filled. Some less well qualified candidates will be admitted because there are fewer applicants from their region.

This is clearly discriminatory: geography and national origin are allowed to override academic criteria. But this sort of discrimination is not morally objectionable. Applicants were not excluded because the region or nation from which they come is viewed with contempt. The exclusion did not show prejudice or contempt; rather, the object was to promote intercultural understanding.

This example shows that the objectionable aspect of racial or ethnic quotas is not that they discriminate. Rather, they are objectionable when (but only when) they show prejudice and/or promote contempt for groups of people.

Quotas for hiring and promotion of visible minorities cannot be viewed as expressing contempt for the white majority. Racial classifications have historically been used to express and promote racial prejudice. The goal of reverse discrimination is the opposite: to promote inter-racial respect and equal opportunity.

Some opponents of reverse discrimination might concede that employing racial quotas is not necessarily wrong, but they might nevertheless oppose such quotas on the grounds that, at this time, they are likely to promote more bad than good consequences. To answer this, the benefits and costs of reverse discrimination must be carefully weighed.

One of the most serious consequences of past (and present) discrimination is that there are practically no native Canadians and very few black Canadians in high positions in government, business and the professions. There are many reasons for this: poverty, inferior schooling, widespread prejudice and exclusion and, in consequence, low self-esteem.

Not all members of non-white minority groups have suffered equally, and some individuals in the white majority have also been burdened with severe disadvantages. Nevertheless, the lack of non-white role models in top jobs has reinforced that non-whites are inferior to whites.

Until there are significant numbers of non-white Canadians in professional and managerial jobs, their absence is certain to reinforce the prejudice of the majority and the low self-esteem of the minority.

Unfortunately, eliminating this discrimination will not, by itself, be enough to solve the problem. Even if all bias against visible minorities were instantly to disappear, it would be decades before the devastating effects of previous bias could be eliminated.

We need to invest in remedial programs for such disadvantaged groups and enable them to achieve better housing, education, health care and so forth. But without reverse discrimination, most of Canada's visible-minority groups will, for the foreseeable future, remain in the lowest socio-economic ranks.

Despite acknowledging these potential benefits, many critics fear that the losses would outweigh the gains.

Does a program of preferential treatment for visible minorities not imply that non-whites are in fact inherently inferior to whites (and so in need of special treatment)? Will preferential hiring and promotion quotas reduce a negative psychological effect on non-whites themselves? (This fear is powerfully expressed by black economist Thomas Sowell: "What all the arguments for reverse discrimination are saying is that black people just don't have it, and will have to be given something.") If unqualified non-whites are hired or promoted to jobs they cannot perform successfully, will their failure not confirm false stereotypes about minority abilities? Will the public not suffer from inferior services as a result of hiring or promoting less-qualified doctors, teachers, social workers or policemen?

Hiring or promoting minority candidates who cannot do the job well would almost certainly be counterproductive. The point of hiring and promotion quotas should be to ensure that competent non-whites are given the opportunity to demonstrate their competence even if, in the fiercely competitive job environment of the present, there may be others (white) with better qualifications.

The evidence is accumulating. Most minority candidates admitted to professional schools under preferential quotas do satisfactory work. Their success is enhancing not only their own self-esteem but the self-esteem of their group. At the same time, it serves powerfully to undermine the majority prejudice that marks them down as inferior.

The evidence suggest that without such quota systems there would be few "success stories"—not because of any racial inferiority but because of inequality of opportunity and deep-rooted (sometimes unconscious) prejudice.

Concepts to consider:

Discrimination, ethnic group, equality of opportunity, majority group, minority group, power, prejudice, race, reverse discrimination, socio-economic status, visible minority.

Of course, there will be disadvantages from a policy of reverse discrimination, including resentment on the part of white job candidates who may see themselves as victims of the quota system.

Preferential quotas are no painless panacea. They will not solve all our racial problems. But in Canada they are probably the most practically effective method of promoting a society or racial equality of opportunity. In short, they are a necessary evil if we are to overcome the barriers erected by generations of prejudice and discrimination.

Paradoxically, if our goal is to break the racial stereotypes and promote a less racially conscious society, we may have to adopt, in the short run, policies that use racial criteria. For this reason we should support the affirmative action proposal of the Special Committee on Visible Minorities in Canadian Society.

The Globe and Mail, Toronto, Monday, June 4, 1984, p. 7.

QUESTIONS

1. Define race.

2. Explain what is meant by visible minority.

3. Define and distinguish between prejudice and discrimination.

4. What are the appropriate criteria for hiring an individual for a paid position? Can these criteria include racial, ethnic, language, or religious criteria? Under what circumstances can they be included in your opinion?

5. Explain "the devastating effects of previous bias." What are the likely affects of prejudice and discrimination on ethnic groups?

6. Explain what is meant by reverse discrimination. What sanctions could be used to enforce reverse discrimination?

7. How does the writer see reverse discrimination as mitigating the effects you cited in answering question (5)?

8. Cite three areas of employment where you feel reverse discrimination should be enforced if it were to become law. Why would these be appropriate areas?

9. Explain equal opportunity. Does reverse discrimination promote equal opportunity?

10. If groups have more than their proportionate share of jobs in a given field of employment, should they be cut down in numbers? Is that what happens, in effect, under reverse discrimination?

FIND A CLIPPING

Find an article that describes an ethnic group with a distinctive culture. Explain, with examples from the article, what is distinctive in this ethnic sub-culture. How can the sub-culture co-exist with Canadian culture? What indications are there of cultural conflict, and how could these be resolved? How can people of this particular ethnic background maintain and reinforce their ethnic identity?

12

Deviance

Deviance refers to actions that are publicly recognized as violating social norms. To deviate is to act in a way that does not conform to social expectations. Sociologists are interested in the social causes of deviant behaviour, in the social circumstances that pressure people to act in ways that are non-conformist, violating the norms which most accept.

Attempting to decide what is deviant frequently provides grounds for a good debate. Three important factors in defining deviance are the extent of agreement that a norm has been violated, agreement about the harmfulness to the group of the action, and the severity of the punishment for it. There is widespread agreement, for example, that murder is a very serious violation of a norm, and that if it is allowed to go unpunished, the consequences for group safety would be serious. Similarly vigilante actions do not receive wide approval, except where the law has broken down. Such acts as prostitution, or getting drunk in public, or obtaining an abortion, arouse debate because the norms that have been violated are less clear, and it is questionable whether the impact of the action on society as a whole is negative. Such actions as dressing in outlandish clothes or dying your hair an unnatural colour may be termed deviant by some, but are not regarded as serious deviations because they do not harm others in the society.

Which acts are labelled deviant may also depend on the time, the place, and the cultural context in which they occur. What may be considered deviant in one situation may not be considered so in another. Jeans, track shoes, and talking and laughing loudly are all out of place at a funeral, but quite appropriate in school. Different cultural groups may interpret the same action differently. Many religious groups in Canada view abortion with abhorrence, while in some other cultures it is an acceptable means of birth control.

Attempts to control deviance involve both formal and informal sanctions. Formal sanctions consist of the legal penalties under the law, "official" punishments such as excommunication by the church, expulsion by a group for violation of their rules, being dismissed from a job because of failure to comply with the requirements for employment, being expelled from school, a court-martial, or dishonourable discharge from the armed forces. Those in positions of authority have the right to sanction those under them for violating the rules that come under their jurisdiction.

Informal sanctions are those imposed by others in the group who associate with the individual judged deviant. Dropping friendships, ostracizing a person, staring, frowning, expressing distaste all carry a message of disapproval and may serve to bring individuals "back into line" as well as deter others from following their example.

The primary method of preventing deviance and ensuring conformity is through the socialization process. In the course of growing up in society, children and young people learn to accept the social norms. However, socialization for many is not a smooth process. They may not learn what is expected, or may be socialized into deviant activities. In addition, normative standards change over time; what is considered right for one generation may not seem so self-evident to the next. Finally, people are not puppets; for reasons of their own, or because of the circumstances in which they find themselves, individuals may choose non-conformity.

Functionalist theorists have argued that deviance may in some instances be functional for society in that it clarifies or redefines the norms, and reinforces them or leads to necessary changes. It can also be argued that both deviance itself, and the enforcement of social control, can create employment (imagine how many people would be unemployed if there were no crime).

Conflict theorists have commonly stressed that the definition of deviance is imposed by those in power, and consequently those without power are most frequently defined as deviant. Symbolic interactionists pay attention to the ways in which deviance is learned from others.

Media coverage of illegal acts often sensationalizes the action, rarely examining in detail all the pertinent background or its causes, whether personal choice or social circumstances. Reporting may reflect the current social definition of deviance, reinforce it, or—in rare instances—serve to change the definition.

Curbing Deviant Careers

INTRODUCTION

While some would argue that prostitution is not a serious deviant act and that adult women who are prostitutes should not be prosecuted, few would argue in favour of under-age females being engaged in prostitution. At present there is no effective way of dealing with the problem. Young girls starting as prostitutes are beginnng a deviant career from which it will be very hard for them to escape.

A large number of probable causes are cited in this article. It is known that many prostitutes were initally victims of sexual abuse within their own families. Because few girls who run away have any means of supporting themselves, many turn to prostitution as a way of making a living. The education system, the economic system, public apathy, the legal system, and the political system can all be faulted for contributing to young girls turning to prostitution.

Voluntary agencies such as the YWCA perhaps have more flexibility than established government agencies for working towards solutions to the problem. Their mandate involves serving the needs of women, and they can act with reasonable speed; using mainly volunteer labour and available resources, they are less costly; the agency is accountable only to their own board of directors. They are freed from the bureaucratic control and public accountability that slows and constrains government action.

Child prostitutes need shelter — brief

By Lorraine Locherty

Edmonton needs residential shelters for child prostitutes, says a brief to the Fraser Commission prepared by the Young Women's Christian Association (YWCA).

The YWCA is considering forming a citizens' committee to look into establishing a shelter for 12- to 16-year-old runaways, says the report, which quotes from a child prostitution series published in February by The Journal.

"For the child who has been involved in prostitution, returning home is rarely possible," the report says.

"We would therefore recommend that shelters and drop-in centres be established for runaway juveniles living on the street who are vulnerable to the temptation of prostitution."

Jeannie Bodnaruk, who works in the YWCA residence office, said Tuesday the organization believes prostitution is a serious problem.

"It's pretty obvious there are a lot of girls working opposite the Y (at 10305 100th Avenue)," said Bodnaruk, who helped prepare the 30-page brief sent last week to the federal commission investigating prostitution and pornography.

"We've taken in the odd juvenile. If the Y can help divert the whole (prostitution) process, or provide protection, we will."

The Youth Emergency Shelter on the South Side helps older teenagers but there are no halfway houses in the city for children.

The YWCA brief points out the link between prostitution and sexual abuse against children.

It recommends increasing sexuality education in the school system and more public awareness programs to combat child abuse.

Police and the courts should make a greater effort to prosecute pimps and customers, the YWCA believes.

"While recognizing the difficulty of getting (child) prostitutes to testify against their procurers or customers, we believe that identifying such persons and exposing them at least to social censure may have a deterrent effect."

Stronger enforcement legislation against non-custodial parents who won't comply with maintenance orders is needed because many of the children who resort to prostitution to provide for their basic needs are from single-parent families, the brief says.

It recommends changes to Alberta's child welfare laws to increase aid to child prostitutes.

"Through our interviews with workers in the field, it became apparent that institutionalizing juveniles involved in prostitution is not a satisfactory solution and at best only a temporary deterrent. Yet institutions are the only secure placement available through the child welfare system."

The Edmonton Journal, May 30, 1984, p. B3.

Concepts to consider:

Deterrant, deviant act, deviant career, education, family, labelling, social control, stigma, voluntary organization.

QUESTIONS

1. What determines whether an act is regarded as deviant?

2. Are prostitutes deviant? Are child prostitutes deviant?

3. List the causes noted in the article of young girls becoming involved in prostitution. What other causes could you add to the list?

4. Explain how one of the causal factors you noted could contribute to a young girl's turning to prostitution.

5. Use some insight, how could you have supported yourself if you had left home at 12, 13, or 14 years of age?

6. What is meant by "deviant career"? What reinforces the continuation of a deviant career?

7. What methods of attempting social control are cited in the article? Why are they ineffective?

8. What are the solutions proposed by the YWCA? Could these provide a means of social control which is more effective than present efforts at control?

9. Name three voluntary organizations or government agencies in your area that help deviants of various kinds. How do these organizations help people shed the stigma of deviance?

Changing the Social Perception of a Deviant Act

INTRODUCTION

The questions on the editorial "Total War on Drunk Drivers" are designed to make you think about ways of changing public attitudes towards drinking and driving. Alcohol has an established place in our culture as a symbol of hospitality and celebration. It is extensively used for pleasure and for the supposed relief of stress. What constitutes alcohol abuse is so ill-defined that negative sanctions are not imposed or are generally ineffective.

Cars are a major means of transportation, and in areas without public transport, the only means. They are also symbols of economic and social status. It seems inevitable, then, that people will drink and drive... or so many believe. Driving while intoxicated is an offence under the criminal code, yet few people take breaking this law very seriously. This editorial comments on the current effort in Nova Scotia to change people's attitude towards having a few drinks and then driving and hoping they will "get away with it." The seriousness with which the majority view intoxicated drivers needs to change so that those who would drive will not drink.

Total war on drunk drivers

The provincial government's war on those who drink and drive continues to gain impetus. A task force of 12 members established to consider all aspects of the matter and to make recommendations to the authorities has had its first meeting. Made up of representatives of government departments, police forces, highway safety lobbyists and members of the medical profession, the task force already is looking at statistics with a view to identifying various facets of the total problem as a prelude to proposing corrective courses of action.

The group, for example, is looking at the possibility of raising the legal drinking age from 18 to 21, a move already taken in some American states in an effort to curb the unacceptably large number of highway accidents involving drinking teen-agers.

The provincial government is moving quickly. A first act was to apply stiffer sentences against those convicted of impaired driving. With that, it undertook to equip police departments with breathalyzer equipment to enable the police to deal quickly with offenders.

Not stopping there, the authorities are progressing in their campaign to enlist educational propaganda in the shaping of attitudes. The drinking driver is no longer viewed by the people of this province as socially acceptable. A general antipathy is developing which the government is seeking further to cultivate. As growing numbers accept the idea that drinking and driving do not mix and must not be mixed, an important step will have been accomplished toward making our highways safer.

As a publicity gimmick, bumper stickers are being made available which read, "Drunk drivers get caught in Nova Scotia." Whatever one may think of bumper stickers, it must be admitted that this could be an effective device in reminding those who drive of the responsibility which is upon them.

The task force is being given the authority to explore every area of the matter. It is not to be restricted in its search for understanding and answers. Hopefully, its recommendations will receive full official attention.

One can have nothing but praise for the concerted effort being made to rid the roads of the drinking driver. Praise, too, is merited by Attorney-General Ron Giffin for his determined leadership. It will be a great day when Nova Scotians are able to say that their highways are free of the threat to safety of those who drink and drive.

The Chronicle-Herald, Halifax, Friday, July 27, 1984, p. 6.

Concepts to consider:

Criminal code, deviance, education, law, mass media, moral entrepreneur, norms, norms of evasion, propaganda, resocialization, sanctions, social control.

QUESTIONS

1. Explain how actions come to be defined as deviant.

2. What are the norms relating to drinking? Are these norms in conflict with one another? How is the violation of these norms sanctioned?

3. Explain what is meant by norms of evasion. Are these applicable to drinking and driving?

4. Explain what is meant by moral entrepreneur. Who are the moral entrepreneurs mentioned in this article?

5. Could raising the drinking age from 18 years to 21 years be effective in reducing the number of accidents involving this age group? Explain why or why not. Take into account the norms and sanctions that relate to young adults and drinking and driving.

6. What types of social control are discussed in this editorial to reduce accidents due to drunk driving?

7. The solutions proposed in this editorial to curb drunk driving include educational propaganda. Are education and propaganda the same (check the dictionary)? Do you consider either or both appropriate solutions? Explain your reasons.

8. Could the press assist in reducing drunk driving? How?

9. Discuss briefly one theory of deviance that could explain why people drink and drive.

FIND A CLIPPING

Protest groups are commonly in the news. A public demonstration is seen as a good way of getting people's attention focused on an issue.

In the course of a public demonstration the group's supporters may violate many norms. Many protests involve civil disobedience; some become violent.

Find a clipping that describes deviance perpetrated in the course of a protest against some existing social arrangement. Explain the issue, describe the action, and the norms broken. Assess whether this action is likely to be effective or not, and why. What is the role of the press in aiding or working against the protesters? Does the report of the deviant actions in the press convey social approval or disapproval? How does it do so?

13

Social Inequality

Despite periodic recessions, Canada is an affluent society with a high standard of living. Yet there are still great disparities in the distribution of wealth and income within this country.

A widely held belief is that Canada offers equality of opportunity, that is, an equal opportunity for all who are able and who are willing to work hard to gain the social rewards that most people are presumed to want, namely wealth, power and prestige. However, in practice there are significant barriers to achieving these for many people because of their class, or because of the status otherwise ascribed to them.

The current distribution of social rewards is often justified by widely held ideologies. These ideologies are sets of beliefs and attitudes that legitimate inequalities by appearing to explain them and make them seem reasonable.

Ideologies are rarely stated explicitly; they are most often implied in statements made about the ways things are. Or they may be implicit in statements made about social life, statements that are widely accepted and rarely closely examined.

Inequality is built into our society in such a way that individuals are not only denied access to social rewards but that inequalities are also passed on from generation to generation. The children of poor families, for example, start life economically and educationally disadvantaged compared with the children of middle-class families. Children and grandchildren of wealthier families have access to opportunites as they grow up that are not available to the poor.

Many theories have been advanced to explain social inequality. Conflict theory was summarized briefly in the introduction to Section 1.

Marxist conflict theorists identify the economy as the base on which the structure supporting inequality rests. It follows that only by altering the capitalist economic mode of production can the distribution of rewards be changed. Functionalist theory (also summarized in the first section) explains inequality in terms of collective benefits to the society. Unequal rewards provide incentives to individual effort, thereby ensuring that the most capable person fills each of the most important, and functionally necessary, positions in society.

The theoretical approaches above have been subject to many criticisms. Max Weber, reacting to Marx, drew attention to the multi-dimensional character of inequality in stressing class, status, and power as the bases for inequality. Other, later writers have advanced both theoretical and empirical evidence to show the weaknesses in both the conflict theories, and the conservative functionalist explanation for social inequality.

You should be aware that underlying many theories are value judgements as to how societal rewards should be distributed and what the implications of such distribution would be for the quality of life of people within the society.

The first article in this section gives some details of the control levied over large corporations, by a few very wealthy individuals and families. The second article looks at an organization created to be more efficient in providing stop-gap help for some of the extremely poor people in the nation's capital. The third article deals with provisions made for the physically handicapped to enable them to participate on more equal terms in everyday activities.

The Economic Elite and Power

INTRODUCTION

Under corporate capitalism, individuals can invest their wealth by buying shares in corporations. The Toronto Stock Exchange is the largest stock exchange in Canada. The Toronto Stock Exchange composite index is based on the value of the shares in the 300 largest companies traded on the Exchange and is used to measure the level of share prices. The concentration of wealth in Canada can be measured by the ownership of the shares of companies traded on the TSE. It is a reasonable measure, although it does not include all corporate wealth. Some companies are completely privately owned. The T. Eaton Company, for example, and Olympia and York Developments Ltd. mentioned in the article are privately owned and therefore not publicly traded on the stock exchange.

Common-share ownership gives shareholders a vote on how the company is managed, as well as a share of the profits. In addition, shareholders who own a large block of the outstanding shares in a corporation can effectively control the company, especially if the remaining shares are widely held by many smaller shareholders. The large shareholders in these companies have control over the company and its subsidiaries and thus very considerable power and influence in the business world.

Corporate capitalism is credited with encouraging enterprise and initiative in developing new ideas and starting new companies. But, as this article shows, in practice large fortunes are more often made through buying shares and gaining control of other companies than by creating, developing and producing new goods and services.

The questions are designed to focus on the effect that the concentration of a "big chunk of business in the hands of a few" might have on social inequality.

Report On Business
Big chunk of business in hands of a few

By Dan Westell

Big business frequently seems faceless, owned by institutions and run by professional managers. But ultimately, share certificates belong to people, and a surprisingly large chunk of Canadian business is dominated by very few.

Some sectors are concentrated in so few hands that all the controlling shareholders would not make a noticeable difference to the lineup in a bank on a typical Friday afternoon.

Taking only the companies that make up the Toronto Stock Exchange's 300 composite index, at the end of June, nine super-rich families or individuals owned shares with a market value of more than $9-billion out of a total index value of about $80-billion.

But even this understates the families' hold on corporate

Canada on at least two counts.

First, Olympia and York Developments Ltd. of Toronto, the largest holding of the Reichmann family, is not listed on the stock exchange. Other families also have private interests, and some have significant holdings in companies that are listed on the TSE but are not included in the 300 index.

Second, and more important, the actual value for the TSE 300 shares directly held understates the extent of the families' influence, because control of a company often rests with a relatively small holding. The market value of all shares in TSE 300 companies in which the same group of nine held a majority, plurality or more than 20 per cent was about $37-billion, or almost half the value of the 300 index.

If the $10.7-billion value of the big five chartered bank shares is removed from the TSE 300 value, because the law limits holdings of bank shares to less than 10 per cent, the nine families held sway over more than half the value of the 300 shares.

Corporate concentration was perceived to be a major problem a decade ago, and then prime minister Pierre Trudeau followed the time-honored Canadian tradition of appointing a royal commission. The report of the Royal Commission on Corporate Concentration, published in 1978, basically concluded that big was not necessarily bad.

But the Bryce report, named after chairman and civil servant Robert Bryce was quite bloodless—it rarely looked behind the companies and industries it analyzed to find the owner's faces.

It overlooked concentrations of individual or family power, in part because a company taking over its main competitor and a family extending its influence into a new field are viewed differently.

The first situation presents a problem in terms of classic economic theory. In a market with many competing players, consumers benefit; in a market with one or a few players, unless it is regulated, companies benefit. In contrast, the problem, if any, when a few people have extensive holdings in a variety of industries is more one of politics than of economics.

It may be a "bad thing" that so much business is concentrated in so few hands, but discussions of that situation are discussions about power, not about the cost or benefits of monopoly or competition.

Corporate concentration, at least prior to the Bryce report, was viewed as a bad thing. A concentration of many businesses in few hands may also be a bad thing, but the report unintentionally points out a major mitigating factor.

Some of the nine family groups that dominate the TSE 300 today did not rate a reference in the Bryce report, or were mentioned only in passing. That indicates there can be considerable turnover at the top of the heap. And even among companies that were considered major forces, control quite often has changed hands.

For example, Edward and Peter Bronfman, through Edper Investments Ltd. of Toronto, and Charles, Edgar and their two sisters, through Cemp Investments Ltd. of Montreal, may be the best known business family in Canada today. Yet Cemp rated only a passing mention in the Bryce report, in the context of a separate report on Cadillac Fairview Corp. Ltd. of Toronto, and Edper was apparently invisible.

Brascan Ltd. of Toronto was the subject of a separate study, but that was before it was taken over by Edper and became a part of the Bronfman empire. Argus Corp. Ltd. of Toronto also rated a study but, again, that was before it became the centre of a group headed by Conrad Black.

CANADIAN FAMILY STOCK HOLDINGS

FAMILY	TSE STOCK HOLDINGS		MAIN COMPANIES
	MARKET VALUE ($ BILLION)	VALUE OF CONTROLLED COMPANIES ($ BILLION)	
THOMSON	2.3	3.8	INTERNATIONAL THOMSON THOMSON NEWSPAPERS HUDSON'S BAY
BRONFMAN (CEMP)	2.0	5.0	SEAGRAM CADILLAC FAIRVIEW
DESMARAIS	1.4	12.9	POWER CORP. CANADIAN PACIFIC CP ENTERPRISES
BRONFMAN (EDPER)	1.0	9.8*	BRASCAN NORANDA TRIZEC LABATT
REICHMANN	1.0	0.6**	HIRAM WALKER ABITIBI
WESTON	0.7	1.3	GEORGE WESTON LOBLAWS
BLACK	0.3	1.1	ARGUS DOMINION STORES NORCEN
SOUTHERN	0.2	1.9	ATCO CANADIAN UTILITIES
SEAMAN	0.2	1.1	BOW VALLEY

*ALTHOUGH THE REICHMANNS OWN ALMOST 50% OF COMPANIES THAT HOLD TRILON AND RELATED COMPANIES, CONTROL RESTS WITH EDPER BRONFMANS; **EXCLUDES HIRAM WALKER RESEARCH: SARON FRIESE

Concepts to consider:

Capitalism, conflict theory, economy, elite, functionalism, ideology, influence, partrilineage, power, social class, status, wealth.

Canadian Pacific Ltd. of Montreal, its investment arm, Canadian Pacific Enterprises Ltd. of Calgary, and Power Corp. of Canada, Montreal, were also covered in separate studies, but at the time, they were not affiliated. Since then, Paul Desmarais has expanded from his base in Power to take a plurality position in CP Ltd., which has given him influence over billions of dollars of stock in CP Ltd. and CPE.

George Weston Ltd. of Toronto, controlled by the Weston family, was alone among the currently dominant corporations rating a separate study for the Bryce commission. The holdings of the Southern, Seaman and Thomson families were not studied separately, even though today the Thomsons would recieve the most—more than $2.3-billion—from a sale of their TSE-listed shares.

But among the families they are far from first in a ranking of total value of shares controlled. There seems to be, for lack of a better phrase, a generation gap among the families, with leverage forming the line.

Among the older family fortunes, second generation or more, such as the Thomsons, the Cemp Bronfmans and Westons, the value of the shares in companies controlled by the family is close to the value of the shares owned. In other words, only rarely is control exercised through a long chain of companies.

On the other hand, pyramiding by owning a part of a company that owns a part of another company and so on, has enabled the Edper Bronfmans and Paul Desmarais to build empires from relatively small starts. This technique seems to be favored by the newer-monied families.

The fact that relatively new entrants can reach the winner's circle tends to weaken any idea of a modern day family compact. The groups that dominate the TSE 300 in some ways reflect the changing composition of Canada as a whole. Among the top nine, three, at most, could be described as established, eastern Anglo money. Three families are Jewish, and one is francophone (although all are eastern), while two come from Alberta.

On the other hand, the current concentration of corporate power illustrates a frequent criticism of Canadian business. Much of the wealth represented has been accumulated by acquisition and the manipulation of companies, rather than by innovation, and the production and sale of goods and services.

Economists have argued that rearranging assets should not be confused with the creation of wealth by starting or expanding an enterprise. But among those who count their fortunes in numbers too large for the human mind to grasp, it is hard to argue with success.

The Globe and Mail, Toronto, Saturday, August 25, 1984, p. B1.

QUESTIONS

1. Define capitalism.

2. Explain what is meant by elite. Are the individuals named in the article part of an elite?

3. How could wealthy individuals/families like those named in the article acquire their wealth?

4. What do these wealthy few actually have control over? How do they exercise control?

5. Define power. Do "the few" have power? What does their power enable them to do?

6. How is this power and influence restrained? Or is it?

7. Explain the statement in the article "...the problem, if any, when a few people have extensive holdings in a variety of industries is more one of politics than of economics."

8. Is the concentration of economic power likely to be dangerous or beneficial to the welfare of Canadians? On what criteria could you decide?

9. Given the concentration of wealth in the hands of a few people, is it possible for the government to make radical changes to alter the distribution of wealth? Is the government likely to try? Why or why not?

Examining the Necessity of Poverty

INTRODUCTION

This article discusses how the distribution of food to the destitute is becoming formalized. The need exists in Ottawa, as in other Canadian cities, to provide emergency food aid to the poor, either by providing meals or by providing groceries free. Combining the efforts of 17 agencies would make the collection and distribution of surplus food to the needy more systematic. However, underfunding makes the existence of Provisions Ottawa problematic. Think about the connection between the underfunding and the status of the recipients of the food.

Poverty in an affluent society like Canada persists. Is poverty functional for the society? Are there affluent groups who actually benefit from the existence of the poor?

Group running food bank for poor needs funds

By Jacquie Miller

A group trying to collect and distribute groceries for the poor has its warehouse but no money to run it.

"We only have $218 in the bank right now," says Matthew Barbour, the paid staffer of Provisions Ottawa, a group trying to set up a food bank in the city.

The group was formed by 17 agencies operating soup kitchens and distributing groceries to the poor, including St. Brigid's soup kitchen in Lowertown and the West End Community Lunch program at Foster Farm Community Centre on Ramsey Crescent.

The agencies distribute about 2,500 free meals a day to the needy.

Ottawa Council agreed to let the group use part of the basement of the former police station on Waller Street as a warehouse until next July, when the city plans to redevelop the building.

But Barbour says they can't move in until they get money for such things as a telephone, insurance, shelves and a cooler.

But he's convinced the food industry and public will be generous with donations of food, money and equipment.

Once the food bank is established, it will accept donations from manufacturers, wholesalers, farmers, grocery stores and the public, then distribute the food to churches and community groups that operate soup kitchens or provide groceries to the poor.

The agencies now solicit food individually. A central warehouse would allow food businesses to donate large quantities of food to be distributed where it's most needed.

As well, people making donations of money or food can be sure it will be passed on to a legitimate group, Ald. Rolf Hasenack says.

Concepts to consider:

Formalization, functionalism, marginality, poverty, power, social class.

The food bank will need about $68,400 for the first six months of operation. A $5,000 grant from the United Way is paying Barbour's salary until November.

Already one wholesaler, who wants to remain anonymous, has agreed to make donations of surplus food, said Barbour.

"If we get one major food chain interested, we'll be well on the way."

In Edmonton, a food bank has been successful, handling about 5,000 pounds of food a day, he said. There, grocery stores have drop boxes where customers donate food.

While the Ottawa group can't take food donations until it has the warehouse set up, money and equipment can be donated by phoning the Ottawa-Carleton Social Planning Council.

The Citizen, Ottawa, Friday, July 20, 1984, p. 37.

QUESTIONS

1. What is the goal of Provisions Ottawa?

2. What are the advantages of having a central warehouse to distribute the food to the various agencies? Think of other reasons not mentioned in the article.

3. Does Provisions Ottawa's idea for the collection and distribution of food parallel what is done by large grocery chains? How is it similar; how is it different?

4. Why isn't Provisions Ottawa generously funded by government and/or big business?

5. How do people in Ottawa come to the point where they need free meals and food handouts?

6. Explain what is meant by "marginality"? Are the recipients of free food "marginal people"?

7. What kind of roles give people power or influence? Explain why. What sources of power or influence do the people receiving free food have?

8. In what ways can the existence of soup kitchens and other services to the very poor be functional to society?

Inequality of Opportunity for the Physically Handicapped

INTRODUCTION

Discussions of inequality usually focus on a concern with the inequitable distribution of power, wealth and income, and prestige. But social inequality can also include inequality of opportunity. One category of people who frequently have difficulty participating in the social and economic activities are the physically handicapped. The physical barriers that restrict their access to places of work, to stores, to public buildings offering services, and places to go for social activities that we all enjoy—restaurants, bars, arenas, theatres, movie houses—also generate economic and social inequalities for the handicapped.

Sudbury's Accessibility Guide lists places in Sudbury according to their accessibility. Substantial gains have been made in recent years in improving access to public places, but your own observation will show you that there are still many barriers for people who have a physical handicap.

The article and the Accessibility Guide refers to those in wheelchairs, the visually impaired and the hearing impaired, but there are a wide variety of physical handicaps, not all of which are readily apparent. Those with chronic lung disease, heart conditions or arthritis, for example, benefit from such conveniences as handicapped parking that is level with doorways, and easy access to elevators.

The questions following the article direct you to explore why buildings are not designed for easy access by all people.

New guide pinpoints problems

The Sudbury Ability Coalition has just completed a Sudbury Accessibility Guide, which provides information on the accessibility of businesses and facilites in Sudbury to the physically disabled.

The Guide is part of the Coalition's Aware Sudbury Project, which is funded through the federal government's Summer Canada Works program.

Leslie Bartoli, project manager of Aware Sudbury, says the purpose of the guide is to provide information on accessibility to the physically disabled and the elderly. "It's a fingertip guide to make things easier for physically disabled and elderly people—so they can judge the accessibility of places before they get there. We don't want them to go out somewhere and then discover they can't use the washroom or the telephones.

To compile the information for the Guide, Bartoli and her workers conducted a telephone survey of 711 public places in Sudbury. They surveyed such places as government and public service agencies, retailers, churches, restaurants, banks and motels and hotels.

The group surveyed the buildings in terms of accessibility of public telephones, parking, the entrance and interior of the building, washrooms, braille assistive devices and hearing-impairment devices.

In the Guide accessible is defined as "A person in a wheelchair (who) can move throughout the specified area independently. An area or facility labelled accessible must comply with the specification of the Ontario Building Code, Section 10."

For example, the Bell Grove Arena was deemed accessible in terms of the entrance, interior, washrooms and parking. However, the telephones were considered inaccessible and the arena has no braille assistive or hearing-impairment devices. The City Centre is listed as being accessible in the areas of parking, entrance, interior and telephones. But the City Centre's washrooms are considered inaccessible and there are no braille assistive or hearing-impairment devices available.

The Sudbury Ability Coalition funded the Guide. Seven hundred copies were printed at a cost of $1.40 per book.

According to Bartoli, accessibility for people in wheelchairs

Concepts to consider:

Attitudes, influence, politics, social inequality, social interaction, values.

has improved in the last 10 years. "A lot of progress has been made in the last 10 years. The intention of the building owners is good—if there were more government grants to assist them, most would have very accessible facilities."

She adds: "Accessibility for people in wheelchairs has come a long way, but there's still a lot that must be done for the visually and hearing impaired."

But Bartoli says she was pleased that most people surveyed were conscious of the accessibility barriers facing the physically disabled. "Overall people were quite conscious and aware of accessibility for the physically disabled and elderly."

Copies of the Sudbury Accessibility Guide can be obtained free of charge from the Coalition office on the seventh floor of St. Andrew's Place, Suite 1. Persons wishing to receive a copy of the Guide in the mail may contact the Coalition. There wil be a cost of $2 for copies sent through the mail, to cover, postage and handling.

Northern Life Weekender, Sudbury, Saturday, August 18, 1984, p. 1.

QUESTIONS

1. Define or describe what the term handicapped means to you.

2. What are the usual assumptions about people's physical abilities underlying the design of buildings, entrances, hallways, access to floors, washrooms, telephones, drinking fountains, furniture etc.?

3. What needs to be changed in these assumptions to allow mobility to the physically handicapped?

4. Should older buildings be adapted to provide for the handicapped? Should new buildings be designed with the handicapped in mind? What values underlie your answers?

5. "The intention of the building owners is good—if there were more government grants to assist them most would have very accessible facilities." Examine this statement. Why are government grants necessary to persuade building owners to make facilities accessible?

6. The physically disabled may have difficulty in gaining access to buildings and using services that the rest of us take for granted. Is this unequal treatment? Explain your answer.

7. What impact is there likely to be on individuals perception of themselves if they cannot use public buildings because of their physical limitations? Explain.

8. Analyse your answer to question (1). Is a degree of social inequality explicit or implicit in it?

9. Does publishing the Sudbury Accessibility Guide do anything to change attitudes towards the handicapped? How? Explain.

FIND CLIPPINGS

Over a one-week period, collect all the clippings you can from Canadian newspapers and magazines relating to people with low incomes. The articles can be on individuals or groups. Is it simple or difficult to find a reasonable number of articles? What does your search tell you about the coverage given by the press to poverty or low-income groups?

Out of the articles you collected, select a maximum of four and answer the following questions: How many reasons are given in the articles for the low incomes of these people? Are the reasons given attributed to the social or economic environment, or to the individual, or both?

Explain the social values and ideology implicit or explicit in the reports.

14

Marriage and the Family

Social institutions are part of the patterns of living that prevail in society. The concept of a social institution labels a part of social life that appears to exhibit order and continuity. The family, the economy, and mass media are examples.

Beliefs and values about what is appropriate and normal are centred around these important areas of social life. Living patterns are guided by the traditions and social expectations that are passed on from generation to generation. People playing roles (mother, wage earner, priest, politician) related to these key areas are guided in their social interaction by social expectations, beliefs, and values.

Change does take place in all institutionalized areas. Change is usually gradual and often meets some resistance. Traditions die slowly, but social expectations are modified over time. Radical transformations are hard to achieve. Changes are often defined as problems because they represent disruptions in the established order. Indeed, difficulties may be created for individuals because the institutionalized guidelines in the form of a clear set of norms, values, and beliefs are no longer clear or do not fit the prevailing circumstances.

The first social institution discussed here is that of the family. Despite considerable variation between families—owing to variations in sub-cultures, religious beliefs, ethnic background, and social class—there is still enough of a common pattern to enable us to say what is typical of the Canadian family.

The traditional form of the family—husband, wife and their children—exists as an institutionalized norm, an ideal to which all families are expected to measure up. Families that are not "conventional" in their structure—single-parent families, families with other relatives living with them, unmarried mothers, unmarried couples living together, parents who both work, childless couples—all confront problems created by social assumptions about what "the family" is "supposed" to be.

The institution of the family is constantly evolving and is now undergoing considerable change. Consequently, many individuals feel tension in their family relationships. The continuing movement toward equality for women in society is one source of change. Women working and the economic need for most families to have two incomes is another.

Social institutions have to mesh with each other. The lack of adaptation in other institutionalized areas to changes in the family creates difficulties. Other institutionalized areas, for example the education system and the economy, operate as if the two-parent family is the norm, and as if in all families the father is the wage earner while the mother stays at home. The schools, for example, both in hours of operation and in the expectations of the teaching staff, often appear to assume that mothers are at home. Women in the labour force face a constant struggle to balance the worlds of home and paid work.

Despite a high divorce rate, which illustrates the pitfalls of marriage, marriage remains popular. Love is the socially legitimate and accepted reason for getting married and for continuing in a marrige. The belief is strongly held that the family is the place where expressive needs can be met and all family members can receive emotional support. In practice, neither marriage nor family life always works out this way, and the violation of the belief (the sense that this is not the way it is meant to be) adds to the heartache of broken marriages or family crises.

As you deal with the articles and questions that follow, reflect on the institutionalized beliefs and values that centre around the family, and on the reality for many families.

The three articles that follow examine current variants on the pattern of finding a partner, getting married and establishing a family.

Dating, Romance and Marriage

INTRODUCTION

Singles clubs have been started in many places to provide an opportunity for single people to meet and socialize. They provide organized social events of all kinds. For some members the aim may be to get to know people of the opposite sex, but for many it is to find some friendship and companionship and enjoy the social activities.

Singles clubs address the problem that many unmarried or no-longer-married people face: the lack of opportunities for making new friends. Single people are often not invited to gatherings by their married friends or, if invited, feel out of place. For more mature people who do want to meet members of the opposite sex, the dating approach used by young adults does not feel appropriate. There are few places for meeting new people. Those that do exist, a bar for example, make some unescorted women feel unsafe.

The writer of this article, observing the scene that he describes, has taken a romantic view of the events, one that reflects a significant theme in the public view of single people and their involvement in social activities. Is this an appropriate view?

Bright, fun-loving, attractive seeks same

By David Macfarlane

"Look, Marshall," says Harold, "they want to get them dancing now." Harold is the president of Celebration Disc Jockey Services. Marshall, the D.J., nods, takes *The Hurting* off, and puts *Guilty*, the Barbara Streisand-Barry Gibb album, on the turntable. He hits the button for the revolving coloured lights. "Yeh," says Harold, "stuff like that."

Bright, fun-loving, attractive, Helen smiles at the man who joins her. "People think only rejects come to things like this." Helen has swimmable brown eyes. "Do I look like a reject?"

Attractive, intelligent, recently separated, Beth is sitting at the same table as Helen in the Commonwealth Room of Toronto's downtown Holiday Inn. She is wondering whether she has the nerve to ask the gentleman standing between the hot trays of deep-fried seafood and the ticket table for the cash bar to dance. Beth is forty-two and as nervous as a schoolgirl. A red candle flickers at the centre of the white cloth on the round table—one of the two dozen red candles, white cloths, and round tables that surround the parquet dance floor for the "Friends of the Opposite Sex" (FOOS) dance. Beth sips a glass of rye and coke rimmed with red kisses.

Sponsored by the Skills Exchange—a community education organization that has planned, among other things, a symposium on "The Art of Being Single"—the FOOS dance has been designed to help people meet people. Not to put too fine a point on it, loneliness is the reason 120 people have paid the thirty-dollar (for two) registration fee. The way FOOS works is this: you come with an "uncommitted" member of the opposite sex—a brother, a sister, a chum, or even, in some cases, an ex—and then, or so it is hoped, you meet someone else. FOOS avoids the problem of most singles get-togethers: many more women than men.

"Should I?" Beth asks her friend. "What does he look like?" Cheerful, attractive, full-figured, Beth's friend has soft, myopic eyes. She lost her good glasses in Puerto Vallarta and refuses to wear her other pair.

At a nearby table, sincere, intelligent, balding, Warren has asked a dark-haired woman with a slight English accent and potent French perfume to dance. "No thank you," the dark-haired woman says to Warren. "My feet are sore." She arrived with an ex-boyfriend which makes it all feel, she says, "a bit like wife swapping." The ex-boyfriend works with computers. "I spend my days at a terminal," he explains. "I don't meet that many people.

"The point of coming to this," continues the ex-boyfriend, "is to let down the barriers. Everyone has an idea why everyone else is here. In a city people keep their barriers up, but at something like this maybe they'll let them down and meet each other halfway."

Neat, boyish, slim, a man has asked Helen to dance, and Beth has approached the gentleman at the buffet. Her friend can't bear to watch. "Is she doing it?" she asks. Also enjoys dancing but *really* hates singles bars. Beth's friend once became so fed up with life in a couple's world she actually went to a bar. There, a man led her onto the dance floor, took her in his arms, and said, "God. You're built like a brick shithouse."

A lone man with a thin moustache moves from table to table. He wears a leather sports jacket and has lank, dark hair. His opening line—"I know what you want"—has not been a success.

Marshall takes Billy Joel off the turntable. He puts on *Baby, Come to Me*, and hits the button for the swirls of pulsating white lights. "Okay," he announces. "This is a spot dance," Beth has returned. The gentleman, she tells her friend, is very nice. "But he hurt his knee skiing and can't dance too much," Beth and her friend decide to go. Now, the dance floor is crowded.

Come to me, let me put my arms around you.

Baby, can't you see

I'm just so glad I found you . . . .

Harold picks the spot. The woman with the slight English accent and the potent perfume wins a copy of *Thriller*. "I guess her feet aren't so sore anymore," says

the young woman who came with Warren. Warren shrugs philosophically.

Helen and the slim young man are dancing beautifully together. The long fingers of Helen's left hand are wrapped around the nape of the young man's neck. Eventually, he escorts her back to the table. He awkwardly thanks her for the dances, and says good night.

Bright, fun-loving, attractive, Helen sits at her table and watches the remaining couples on the dance floor. Marshall is playing Frank Sinatra's version of *New York, New York*. A few of the candles have gone out. The tablecloths are littered with abandoned glasses. The neat young man with whom Helen was dancing has disappeared through the doors of the Commonwealth Room. The scene reminds her of something. Her expression is wistful. "It looks," she says, "sort of like a wedding."

Saturday Night, August 1984, p. 52.

Concepts to consider:

Marriage, network, norms romantic love, social institution, social interaction.

QUESTIONS

1. List all the reasons you can think of for people to be single.

2. What is wrong with being single? Why do people think that being single is a situation that has to be defended, or corrected? Examine the societal reaction to "singledom" and explain how it affects single men and single women.

3. How do people meet members of the opposite sex? Do not just list the ways, try to categorize them according to the established patterns in our society.

4. Why are singles get-togethers likely to get many more women than men? Explain the social pressures that cause this situation.

5. Do you think it is true that "in the city people keep their barriers up, but at something like this maybe they'll let them down and meet each other halfway"? Explain.

6. How do people "keep their barriers up"? And why might they do so?

7. What do you think is the goal of FOOS?

8. Comment on the adjectives used to describe the men and the women.

9. Comment on the general tone of the article. What is the underlying assumption of the writer? Does it represent a widely held social view?

Changing Norms and Values in Marriage

INTRODUCTION

The institution of marriage is changing as the traditional marriage relationships and patterns are perceived as ill-adjusted to modern social conditions. Marriage contracts have been widely debated. They may be practical but certainly do not seem to fit very comfortably with our romantic view of marriage. What has changed over time to make discussion of a marriage contract to cover the relationships appear appropriate to some couples?

Marriage contracts: not romantic, but very useful

By Doris Anderson

June is still the most popular month for weddings and the trend is back to old-fashioned formal church affairs. But more and more couples are underpinning all euphoria with tough new marriage contracts that define how everything is to be shared from the washing up to who gets the silver should married bliss prove not to be eternal.

With divorce in Canada rising at the rate of 4 per cent a year, by 1990 one in every two marriages will stand a good chance of ending up in the courts. "Because women are so vulnerable in marriage, contracts are really important. They help everyone clarify their expectations," says Shirley Greenberg, an Ottawa lawyer.

Marriage contracts are legal in all provinces and can be used to define all the things that are not defined in the various provincial family law reform acts. The only area that cannot be decided in a marriage contract is the custody of children. The courts still reserve the right to decide that.

Family law reform swept the country in the aftermath of the Irene Murdock case. Irene Murdoch was the Alberta ranch wife who lost out so badly in the courts in 1972 that her case became a rallying cry for a whole generation of women. Through the 1970s, family law acts were passed in province after province.

Women criticized many of the acts because family assets were defined as the house, the cottage, the car; but bonds, stocks, pension plans and other financial assets were not covered. Manitoba, Saskatchewan, Alberta and Quebec give broader definitions of financial assets than the other provinces. The British Columbia and Saskatchewan acts include pension plans under assets.

But in Ontario, which, after Quebec, was the second province to pass family law reform in 1978, men, who have been clever enough to squirrel away assets in paintings for the office, or boats used for office entertaining, and so on, have succeeded in not sharing those assets with wives in divorce actions.

Right now, the Leatherdale case is before the Supreme Court. An Ontario woman who worked and then stayed home to look after a child is suing to get half to the $40,000 of Bell Canada shares that she and her husband accumulated during the marriage for the couple's retirement. The decision will set an important precedent.

A marriage contract, then, should shore up all the holes that might exist in provincial laws, and it works for both partners. A contract should define what each person brought into the marriage, and which, by law, he or she is entitled to take out. Any inheritance during the marriage remains the property of the person inheriting. But all the assets accumulated during the marriage, besides houses, cottages, furniture, cars, (which family law reform acts define) should also be set out—bonds, stocks, and family businesses in which both partners contribute and work.

"Couples begin to shift nervously when I bring up two points while we're discussing marriage contracts," Greenberg says. "When I point out that if a woman stays home to have a baby she not only loses her salary, but she also loses seniority and career opportunities and she should be compensated for that, men get edgy. Then again, if I suggest there should be some protection built into the contract for the woman if the marriage breaks up, by placing a value on her contribution while she stayed home to raise the family—they don't like that either."

According to family lawyers, women should try to get into a contract whether husbands will keep up pension plan contributions and insurance premiums while the woman stays home to look after children. The contract should also set out what kind of contribution the man might make if the woman needs retraining to get back into the work force after staying home.

Marriage contracts can also define how much money a woman is to get should she stay home to run the house. They can even define who takes out the garbage and who gets up in the middle of the night to feed the baby. However, lawyers caution that enforcing penalties for delinquency in household chores is difficult to carry out. Like many other contracts, a marriage contract should be reviewed and renegotiated at set intervals as the situation changes with money and children.

Anyone who thinks a marriage contract is too cold-blooded for a love relationship should think soberly about the fact that in Canada, after five years, 75% of child support payments are not being made. In Ontario alone, child-support payments are $85 million in arrears—and most of the slack is being picked up in welfare payments.

In Canada, it's easy for a man to get out of paying child support and he all too frequently does. Throwing a man in jail is sometimes effective in making him pay for the support of his children, but difficult and expensive for wives to do with no money for lawyer's fees.

Marriage contracts, then, are not hard-nosed and crass devices to sour one of our most cherished and romantic relationships. They are the modern way to give love a little solid help.

Let's face it. What other partnership involving such a commitment in time, energy and emotional and monetary investment would people undertake without any kind of agreement or plan?

The Financial Post, May 29, 1982, p. 8. With permission of the Financial Post.

Concepts to consider:

Family, gender roles, marriage, norms, power, romantic love, social change, social institution.

QUESTIONS

1. Reread the last paragraph of the article. Can you think of another example?

2. What is the basis on which marriage allegedly takes place in Canada?

3. Why might it be a good idea to get "everyone (to) clarify their expectations" by making a marriage contract? Don't people normally enter marriage with clear expectations?

4. What are the perceived inequalities in marriage that marriage contracts should be designed to correct?

5. How did these inequalities come about in the first place?

6. Do these perceived inequalities affect only one spouse? Explain and give evidence to support your answer.

7. Which theoretical perspective would be most appropriate for analysing the process of negotiation involved in making marriage contracts? Explain why.

8. Why can the custody of children not be decided in a contract? Parents are normally responsible for everything with regard to minor children.

9. Can a marriage contract be useful where there are no assets?

10. Are readers of The Financial Post likely to be receptive of this approach to marriage?

11. Draft a marriage contract for yourself and a partner.

Roles Fathers Play

INTRODUCTION

Divorce is now commonplace. The rate of remarriage is also high. This article deals with middle-aged fathers who remarry and have a second family. This is still unusual enough to cause comment, although it is likely to become more common. Consider both the age of the men and the age of their partners and the way in which the reaction of others can make life either easy or difficult for these families. The role of father is a complex one. Think about playing it twice—once when relatively young, and again when older.

Second-family fathers worry less, enjoy more

MONTREAL (CP)—They can change diapers with aplomb, diagnose colic and shrug off the trials of teething. But they worry about staying in shape and surviving to see their children mature.

They are among the growing ranks of middle-aged men fathering their second families, a fraternity with the time and experience to savor the ups and downs of childrearing.

"I've lived through diaper rashes, colic and teething before," says 42-year-old Martin Taylor, whose son Nicholas was born two years ago. "I recognize the difference between teething troubles and the flu.

"Now I worry less and enjoy more."

Taylor, who has two children from a previous marriage, is among the increasing number of middle-aged men who Statistics Canada say are starting second families.

In 40 per cent of 1982 marriages in Canada, at least one partner had been married previously. Half were men.

The older, second-family parent is usually male because women are limited by the biological clock. Men can father children at 50. Women at that age almost never have children.

While second-family fathers have a chance to avoid mistakes made with the children of their first marriage, they also have special problems.

"Usually the second-family father realizes he made some mistakes the first time around and will vow not to repeat them," says psychologist Abe Worenklein. "But many aren't able to take insight and change it into behavior."

Others carry guilt over the effect divorce had on the children of the first marriage. As a result, they may be more permissive with the children of their second. They may also be more involved.

Worenklein says some children are bothered by having a father older than their friends'.

"The 10-year-old boy may want to horse around a lot with his dad," he says. "That can be more difficult when the father is 58 or 60."

Fathers and their children both

Concepts to consider:

Divorce, family, marriage, role, social change, social interaction.

worry about the parent dying before the family is grown.

It made no difference, however, to 57-year-old restaurant owner Shalom Bloom, who has three children with his second wife, Roslyn.

"Under no circumstances would I have left children out of my marriage," says Bloom. "I also wanted Roslyn to have children. I am 15 years older than she is, which means she'll almost certainly outlive me. She should have children against that day."

Bloom said his patience has grown, not declined, with age. The noise and confusion of three active children in the house bothers him less than it did 30 years ago.

"With my first family, I was more inclined to shout at them to be quiet without trying to find out what was going on.

"Today, I find children so easy to talk to, and to reason with. I'm more relaxed and I'm friendlier."

The London Free Press, Monday, June 23, 1984, p. D3. With permission of The Canadian Press.

QUESTIONS

1. What does the role of father entail?

2. Apart from being mistaken for the child's grandparent, what other snags do you see in being an older-than-average father? Use the article plus your knowledge of the social expectations of fathers.

3. What advantages would a father have the second time around? Use both the article and your own insights.

4. Are children of second-time, but older, fathers likely to have advantages or disadvantages? Identify them.

5. Are there more second-family fathers now than in the past? Explain your answer.

6. Are there socially established ways of handling relations between the father's first family and second family? What does your answer imply for these relationships?

7. If you wanted to investigate the attitudes of second-family fathers, as is done to a minor extent in the article, what theoretical perspective would you use?

8. Outline the research methodology you would employ.

FIND A CLIPPING

Find a clipping that relates to difficulties faced by couples in contemporary society, for example, divorce, role reversals, financial matters, living together but not married, childlessness, and children in trouble with the law.

What is the nature of the "problem" discussed in the clipping you have selected? Who defines the situation as a problem?

Who is affected by this problem—the mother, father, children or all individuals in the family? How are they affected?

Does this problem affect many families in society? If so, what does this mean in terms of the institutionalized form of the family as we think of it today?

15

Education

In Canada, much is expected of the education system, both in training people for positions in the economy and social life. Education has become an institutionalized, formal activity in Canada as in other modern industrialized societies. In industrialized societies, going to school is an accepted part of childhood and adolescence, and many people continue with further training. The teaching that takes place in schools, colleges, universities, and in other organized settings provides the knowledge, skills, and social values presumed to be appropriate for adult life.

The education system is influenced greatly by the social, economic and political environment, that in turn also has some impact upon it. It is this interaction which interests sociologists.

The education system fulfills specific functions for Canadian society, as in other industrialized societies. The public and private elementary and secondary schools provide a bridge from the private world of the child's home to the public world of adult life and work. Because education is con-

sidered so important, schooling to a certain age is compulsory under the law and is viewed by the vast majority of people as a crucial part of the socialization process that all young people must undergo. The schools provide the initial training for participation in the labour market, a function that may be completed by university or training college.

Through the education system, children learn the culture of their society and become integrated into a common culture. Giving all young people a common knowledge base is considered especially important where a significant proportion of the population are immigrants. In the context of an officially bilingual country, the issue of language of instruction becomes a contentious one. Other groups may also want their language and culture perpetuated through the school system.

The education system is also linked with the system of stratification. In an open-class society such as Canada, it is considered to be the task of the school system to reward talent and to ensure that pupils' abilities are developed as far as possible. In this way the most talented will be ensured upward social mobility, and society will benefit.

Change is affecting the education system as it is affecting all social institutions. The education system has been criticized because it has failed in practice to alter the disparities created by social class for all but a small number. The tendency is rather to perpetuate the social class standing of the family, especially for the poorest families.

The system is constantly being challenged as to how well it really does prepare students for the labour force. Schools are expected to review their curriculum to put greater emphasis on basics, or science, or whatever is felt to be the current priority. In the next decades, universities are likely to be subjected to a major readjustment, with increasing enrollments and declining budgets the impetus for reform.

With the changes in the labour market, which will lead to career changes for many during their lifetime, and with the rapid rate of change in response to technology, it is highly likely that education will become a lifetime activity. There are already many more mature students in colleges and universities than in past decades. Those who lack schooling or formal training find it increasingly difficult to get work. It may well be that in the future everyone will come to regard education as a lifetime process.

Education does have significance for each and every individual. Many would argue that education is a right; denial of the right to an education robs people of the chance to develop their full potential and of full participation in economic and social life.

The first article in this section focuses on a significant problem: those adults who are functionally illiterate. The second article deals with the content of the school curriculum and the controversy that can be aroused over the issue of content. The third article examines the interaction of politics, the law and education.

Illiteracy—Tackling an Individual and a Social Problem

INTRODUCTION

As this article explains, many adults cannot read and write well enough to cope with everyday living. Yet illiteracy is a hidden problem. Just how many adults are functionally illiterate is hard to measure but a rough estimate is that 1 in 5 Canadian adults has the equivalent of Grade 8 or less (1981 Census). Illiteracy is a cost to the society in terms of the lost potential output. There is also a dollar cost in unemployment and welfare payments. As jobs that do not require literacy skills become fewer and fewer, the illiterate will have increasing difficulty in finding work. Illiteracy is frustrating for its victims and leaves them open to exploitation.

This letter is taken from The Villager, a publication "serving the Community of West Toronto." Publicizing the problem can increase public and voter awareness. The question is how this awareness might be translated into action to provide classes or some other means of increasing adult literacy.

Adult illiteracy alarming

By Doug Little

One of the most serious problems facing our society as we enter the so-called High-Tech era is the serious problem of adult illiteracy.

The 1981 Census brings the problem close to home. Toronto is divided into 142 census tracts of about 4,000 people each. Of these tracts, 35 have almost half of their population reading at less than a grade eight level of education. Grade 9 is the figure used by UNESCO to define the minimum level of functional illiteracy.

The bulk of these tracts define a continuous area running from Bathurst in the East to Bloor and Dundas in the West; from King in the South, to St. Clair in the North. Some quick arithmetic leads to the conclusion that somewhere between 75,000 and 150,000 of Toronto's citizens are functionally illiterate.

Some of these people have come to Canada from other countries where English is not the first language and where formal, publicly financed education ends at Grade 4. A surprising number, however, are people who have made it through school in Ontario without becoming functionally literate.

Such problems often closely reflect patterns of socio-economic inequality. Furthermore, participation in adult basic education programs has frequently been precluded by social and economic barriers.

Can you imagine that 25 per cent of us in Ontario have difficulty reading newspapers, job applications, government job creation notices and regulations, health and safety regulations at work, notices from schools about our children's activities and a majority of the written materials produced by nearly all government and private social agencies. These people are being denied the fundamental right to education as embodied in the United Nations' Universal Declaration of Human Rights, thereby limiting full participation in their places of work, local, provincial or national societies.

Those without functional literacy skills are the most at risk, for in a world where high technology-related skills are one possible key to a new employment, access to the training programs necessary to get into these new fields is restricted to Grade 10 or even Grade 12 graduates. The new National Training Act makes no provision for basic education to help undereducated adults reach these levels.

This exclusion of those whose ideas could most help us and whose economic needs are greatest, strikes at our very ability to find our way out of the downward spirals of unemployment, low productivity and poverty.

Illiteracy, a significant problem by itself, is but one symptom of larger difficulties facing us. These include unjust economic relationships, compounded by a set of social policies and legislation which accept poverty and high unemployment as inevitable.

Concepts to consider:

Class, conflict theory, economy, education, function, government, influence, power, socio-economic status.

Britain launched a government supported literacy effort 10 years ago. Why not Ontario? The obvious lack of support for such a fundamental civic right has led many to wonder who benefits from illiteracy. Some groups must or we would have seen at least a start before now.

As things stand in Ontario, the proportion of the budget allocated to adult Education within the overall budget of the Ministry of Education is *less than one per cent*. The proportion available for literacy within this is just a fraction of the one per cent.

The Toronto Board of Education operates or pays for a number of Adult Upgrading courses through such projects as the City Adult Learning Centre, East End Literacy, and St. Stephen's and St. Christopher's Community Houses. This is clearly only scratching the surface.

As the Chairman of our Continuing Education Committee, I can tell you that we will soon be taking major new initiatives in this area but, owing to financial constraints, there is a limit to what school boards can do.

The Governments of Canada and Ontario must begin to address the problem squarely. There is no excuse for this level of illiteracy in a country as rich as Canada in 1984.

The Villager, Toronto, August 1984, p. 47.

QUESTIONS

1. Explain what is meant by functional illiteracy. How can it be measured?

2. List all the reasons you can think of to explain why people are functionally illiterate.

3. Why is illiteracy a hidden problem?

4. What handicaps do those who are illiterate experience?

5. Explain how "... participation in adult basic education programmes has frequently been precluded by social and economic barriers."

6. Is education a "fundamental right" of the individual in your opinion? Explain your answer.

7. What is the cost to society of having large numbers of functionally illiterate people?

8. Who benefits from illiteracy?

9. How would you teach adults to read and write to a functional level? Suggest solutions that address the problems you listed in answering questions (2), (3), and (5).

10. Who could, and should, pay the dollar bill for literacy programmes? Why?

11. What power, or influence, might Doug Little exercise to find solutions to the problem?

Who Decides What Is Taught in School, and on What Criteria?

INTRODUCTION

One function of education is said to be to equip students for adult life and for participation in the economy. If so, then presumably the content of the curriculum should reflect this. However, the notion of what students need to know for adult life is so broad that there is considerable room for argument over just what specifics students should learn and whether it is the job of the schools or of life experiences to teach them. As this article illustrates, course content that relates to beliefs and values is controversial.

Sociologists who are conflict theorists would argue that education is imposed on students and that generally the ideas and values that are taught support the dominant ideology of the society. Thus they would see the proposal to introduce a course on capitalism and free enterprise economics as only a more blatant example of the process that is always occurring.

Capitalism course causes ruckus

By Don Braid

EDMONTON—In conservative Alberta, education is an issue that makes the blood boil even when there's no summer heat-wave.

Some parents battle any form of publicly funded sex education, protesting whenever their children seem to acquire forbidden knowledge at school, fighting to have "questionable" books removed from school libraries.

For other parents the key issue is religion, or the lack thereof. They vigorously protest the "secular" public school system. They loathe the "humanist" values it teaches. They yearn to replace public schooling with private religious schools that teach, or preach, their own brand of truth.

A committee on tolerance recently found that some private schools flirt dangerously with bigotry. The fundamentalists countered that the real bigots are bureaucrats who tell them what their children are allowed to learn.

To these continuing controversies, the Tory government has now added another—its own wish to turn the public schools into training grounds for little capitalists.

The first hints of this came late last year, when Premier Peter Lougheed said reform of the education system would be a priority in 1984.

He wasn't kidding. In a discussion paper on industrial strategy released recently, his government proposed to fund post-secondary programs that meet the needs of the economy.

The paper didn't say so, but the clear implication was that "impractical" programs will have trouble getting funds.

It seems that Albertans can forget their Chaucer, their Shakespeare, their airy-fairy courses in art, music, and early Celtic pottery. What this government wants is salesmen, managers, computer experts, financial wizards, a great legion of practical people to make the province boom again.

The idea has wide support in the business world. When Lougheed told a chamber of commerce crowd recently that high-school graduates don't understand how the economy works, he got a huge round of applause.

At a press conference later, when a reporter questioned him about why he wanted to introduce courses on "capitalism," he smiled grimly and said he only wanted students to know about "the real world."

Now his education minister, Dave King, proposes that free enterprise economics be taught to the exclusion of other "operating systems."

Concepts to consider:

Capitalism, conflict theory, democracy, education, function, human capital theory, ideology.

King didn't say that the schools can't mention communism, socialism, or other economic systems. But they would only be taught as theories, not as models that apply to the real world. Only capitalism would be taught as an actual working system.

Such a course "would give a greater understanding of how the economic system works," King said. "It's pretty evident, for example, that our high school students come out of the system with virtually no understanding of how credit operates..."

He added that they know little idea about the role of "entrepreneurship" or the importance of equity capital in creating jobs.

King is probably right—many grads don't know how to balance a cheque book, let alone run a business. But the implications of his demand worry even conservative educators.

Ernie Sehn, president of the Alberta School Trustess Association, doesn't have any problem with teaching free enterprise.

"But to suggest that there is a particular right economic strategy and that (is) the only one, I would say is totally inappropriate," said Sehn.

He noted that it's hardly realistic to prepare students to live in a world of competing systems by teaching them about only one.

Then Sehn got to the heart of the matter: "I certainly do not think that the curriculum and the content of the schools should be determined by the party in power at any particular time."

This is nub of the struggle. Educators see the government's plan as political meddling, while the Tories regard it as an overdue effort to bring the educators to heel.

The Tories have felt for years that teachers and school officials are out of touch with the public. They regard the education bureaucrats as a snooty bunch who believe they know what's best for parents and students.

So the Tories want to make them responsive to the "public"—meaning the publicly elected government. They regard this as democracy, not meddling.

The battle is bound to heat up in the coming months as the government orders the education department to develop a course in free enterprise, and many teachers resist the whole idea.

The details for the debate are new, but the controversy over education is as old as the province itself. Albertans would be lost without it.

Winnipeg Free Press, Friday, August 10, 1984, p. 7.

QUESTIONS

1. If you could design a school programme based on your experience in it and in the outside world, what would you include? What criteria did you use as a basis for deciding which subjects to include?

2. Who decides what is taught in school now? Do you think they decide curriculum content on the basis of societal needs, or the individual needs of the children, or both, or on other criteria?

3. Who pays for education? Should those that pay the bill have a say in the choice of curriculum content? Do they now?

4. Should politicians influence the content of education? Explain why you respond as you do.

5. Is teaching capitalism and free enterprise economics a good idea in your opinion? Should students learn about competing economic systems?

6. Could teaching capitalism be termed occupational socialization?

7. Define ideology. Is teaching capitalism teaching an ideology?

8. Give an example of the way in which ideology is taught in school from your own experience.

9. Is it possible to have an ideologically neutral education system? Would such an education system be desirable?

Language and the Perpetuation of Culture

INTRODUCTION

The sociological issue to consider in reading this article is the role of language in perpetuating culture. The language in which children are taught at school is important because it becomes part of the children's culture, and perpetuates the shared culture of the group, in this case, Quebec society.

The Quebec legislature originally passed Bill 101 in 1977 to reverse the decline in the numbers of children attending French schools. Under Bill 101 only those children who had a parent who had been educated in the English schools of Quebec or whose siblings were already in English schools could have an education in English.

Bill 101 was later amended to allow the children of those who moved to Quebec from other provinces to attend English schools provided the sending province granted the right of French education to Quebeckers moving there. Bill 101 was challenged in the Quebec Courts and finally ruled unconstitutional by the Supreme Court.

Court rules Bill 101 'inoperable'

OTTAWA (CP)—The Supreme Court of Canada ruled Thursday that children of Canadians educated anywhere in the country have the constitutional right to an English-language education in Quebec.

The ruling overturns two clauses of the province's Charter of the French Language that restricted Quebec English schools to the offspring of Quebeckers educated in the province.

The court said in its ruling that the Constitution's so-called Canada clause, which guarantees minority language education across the country, is "incompatible" with the Quebec language charter, known as Bill 101 and that the Quebec language law's restrictions on English-language education are "inoperable."

The decision also said that restrictions on English-language education in Quebec "are not legitimate restrictions" under the federal Charter of Rights.

"It is inconceivable that the restrictions that Bill 101 imposes on rights relative to the language of education could have been considered . . . as being confined to 'the limits that can . . . be justified in a free and democratic society,'" the high court said.

Section 23 of the Federal Charter of Rights and Freedoms stipulates that the children of English- or French-Canadians anywhere in the country have the right to an education in their mother-tongue where numbers warrant.

On February 1, the provincial charter was changed to allow English schooling for children coming from provinces where Quebec judges that French-language schooling is equivalent to the educational facilities provided Quebec anglophones.

The ruling concludes a two-year court battle pitting the Quebec Association of Protestant School Boards and the federal and New Brunswick governments against the Quebec government.

The school board association had asked the Supreme Court to decide whether school boards operating English-language primary or secondary schools in Quebec are constitutionally obliged to admit children educated in other provinces.

It also asked if that was so, did the government of Quebec have to provide funding for them as it does for children who qualify for English schools in the province under Bill 101.

The third question asked whether the French-language charter's restrictions "are of no force and effect."

The court only ruled on the first question because written and oral arguments were not made on the others during the proceedings.

The ruling should determine the status of funding for about 400 school children who were attending English-language schools in contravention of Bill 101. The provincial government has refused to provide funding for those children.

The Telegraph Journal, Saint John, Friday, July 27, 1984, p. 1.

Concepts to consider:

Cultural transmission, culture, education, language, law, mother tongue, politics, socialization.

QUESTIONS

1. What percentage of Quebec's population has English as their mother tongue? What percentage of the population has French as their mother tongue?

2. Is the number of French speakers declining in Quebec? Why?

3. Why did the Quebec legislature pass Bill 101?

4. Does education serve to preserve culture? How? How does this relate to the Quebec situation?

5. What do you think might be the result for Quebec culture of the Supreme Court ruling?

6. Why is attendance at school and the language of education covered by law?

7. In your opinion, should parents have a choice on the language of education—French, English, or any other language? Under what circumstances should they have this choice?

8. What are the likely implications for society if parents have a free choice in the language of instruction?

9. How does the language of instruction in school affect families?

FIND A CLIPPING

Education is a social institution that involves almost all young Canadians. While institutionalized areas of the society exhibit continuity, this does not mean that change does not take place. Find an article relating to schools or to post-secondary education in Canada that illustates change in the previously institutionalized pattern.

Discuss what is meant by social institution and apply this concept to the situation in the article. Explain why change is taking place. Is it being resisted, or is there agreement that change is necessary?

16

Religion

Religion involves beliefs oriented towards the sacred or supernatural. These beliefs are held collectively and are reinforced through ritual as in the services in synagogue, church, chapel, or temple. Sociologists do not focus on the content of religious beliefs but on the social aspects of religious life, such as the organization of religious groups, participation in religious groups, and the effect of religious beliefs and activities on life in the community.

Religion is institutionalized in Canadian society, as it is in most societies, and the expression of religious beliefs has become formalized in social patterns of behaviour and activity. We can readily identify buildings where religious activities take place and individuals employed by religious organizations, such as clergy, nuns, and rabbis. Most of us are familiar with the services, prayers, hymns, and psalms that give public expression to religious belief in our communities. There are, of course, many other rituals and occurrences, from meditation to chanting, from speaking in tongues to fasting, from feasting to sacrifice, depending on the form the belief takes.

Like other institutions, religion is not static. When the traditional means of religious expression do not meet the needs of a changing society, new religious beliefs, new ways of expressing old beliefs, and new ways of spreading the message to non-believers and those who doubt come into being. As membership in the older, established churches has been declining, other ways of attracting believers are growing, both within and outside these churches. How religious beliefs find expression reflects the available means within the culture. Knowledge of religion, and religious expression, is promoted via the mass media. There are many thousands of books on religious topics available; religious programming on radio has been around for many decades. Television religious programming makes use of the latest in communication techniques and has expanded steadily in recent decades. It now commands audiences of millions in North America and involves large organizations and millions of dollars. The first article that follows deals with television evangelism in Canada.

The second article focuses on the concerns of a minority religious group. There are only two ways in which religious believers can increase their numbers and ensure perpetuation of their beliefs: by gathering large numbers of converts and by ensuring that their children marry others of the same background and religious faith. Marriages with others of a different religion not only dilutes the faith, it may, if numbers are small, threaten its very survival.

Televangelism as a Religious Alternative

INTRODUCTION

The established churches have traditionally relied on people coming together at regular times for worship. Members of the parish or congregation thereby get to know one another, and think of themselves as members of the church.

However, the established churches either do not reach or do not address the needs of many people. Television evangelism attempts to reach such people and thus appeals to growing numbers. The programme *100 Huntley Street* is a long-lived Canadian evangelical religious programme directed to audiences across a major part of the country.

Television audiences for religious shows are large. What is the appeal? Is it that the evangelical approach, or the fundamentalist beliefs, provide answers to many troublesome questions raised by changes in the larger society—changes that may often appear to threaten traditional lifestyles?

Consider the difference, in presentation and message, between *100 Huntley Street* and other similar religious programming, and the mainline churches. Consider any factors that are common to both.

Electronic scripture aimed at millions

VANCOUVER (CP)—Just one stirring word about a colleague's experiences with Jesus Christ and David Mainse's tears flow like March snow melting off a rooftop.

Mainse is host, star and driving force of *100 Huntley Street*, Canada's only daily television Christian ministry.

Begun in June 1977, as the flagship program of the Toronto-based Christian Communications Inc., *100 Huntley Street* is shown on 26 independent stations across Canada, six affiliates of the Ontario-based Global Television Network, six U.S. stations, and two U.S. satellites.

Crux of each 90-minute program is a hard-sell evangelistic warning that a "personal acceptance" of Jesus Christ as the only true Saviour of humanity is the only ticket to heaven.

Conducted with a talk show format, *100 Huntley Street* consists mainly of guests telling Mainse about their spiritual transformations and the positive personal growth they have enjoyed as a result.

Mainse, an ordained Pentecostal minister, says his organization toes no official line on such traditional fundamentalist bugaboos as abortion, feminism, homosexuality and the removal of prayer and Bible reading from public schools, but representatives of organizations opposed to these causes are frequent speakers on the program.

His television financial pitch ranges from subtle requests for letters of support to unabashed pleading.

Mainse also makes personal appeals for funds at rallies held in cities throughout Canada.

Between September 1980, and August 1981, says communications director Doug Burke, the take was close to $10 million from *100 Huntley Street* contributions alone—up nearly $2.5 million from the 1979-80 total.

Burke says $2.5 million to $3 million is spent annually for air time and production costs on *100 Huntley Street*, 12 other weekly Christian telecasts, including ministries in French, Italian, Greek, German, Portuguese, Ukrainian, Chinese, Spanish and Dutch, and special variety-and-music programs for school-aged children and teenagers.

The rest pays for a 200-plus staff across the country and maintaining the organization's 27 Christian counselling centres.

To answer the telephone calls solicited by Mainse during his daily broadcasts, 1,000 volunteers are available around the clock in the counselling centres and in their homes.

Critics say the program preys on low-income, infirm and uneducated viewers who have little to do each day but watch television.

Burke admits that some of the program's audience may be poor and uneducated—Huntley Street's largest single viewing group is female and over age 54—but "most people tell us it is the obvious sincerity of the program."

It's not the only organization to preach an electronic scripture from a Maple Leaf slant.

A year ago, Christian Life Assembly, an independent evangelical church in Langley, east of Vancouver, began filming half-hour programs shown Sunday mornings on stations reaching 97 per cent of B.C. and parts of the Yukon, and on cable to the northwestern U.S..

Focus on the program is to present personal testimonies by born-again Christians living in or around the Langley area. Interviews are conducted on the street, in the church's prayer lounge or the pastor's study.

Host of the show is the church's pastor, Leroy Lebeck, a large, handsome man with a surprising television savvy after such a comparatively short time in front of the camera.

Lebeck also has a team of counsellors waiting in the wings of his church afer each telecast to answer telephone calls from people wishing to commit themselves to Jesus Christ, but unlike Mainse, doesn't ask his viewers for money.

Only one per cent of the $10,000 the program costs each month comes from unsolicited viewer donations. The rest comes from church coffers stocked by a congregation numbering from 1,500 to 2,000.

The program is to reach the non-church-goer, "the guy in the factory, the guy on the job."

"People want Canadian content. People who are watching this type of program aren't watching the others. They're turned off by too much Hollywood and Madison Avenue."

Terry Winter, a seven-year alumnus of BCTV, whose show has been the station's No. 1 religious broadcast for six years, works on a similar premise.

Broadcast on 10 stations in western Canada and Ontario, his total weekly viewing audience is about 100,000.

Times-Colonist, Victoria, March 6, 1982, p. 21. With permission of The Canadian Press.

Concepts to consider:

Anomie, evangelism, groups, mass media, norms, open group/closed group, religion, ritual, sanctions, secondary group, symbol, voluntary group.

QUESTIONS

1. Why is television used to spread the churches' messages?

2. Define evangelism. Explain the difference between evangelical religion and the major alternative Protestant denominations.

3. Religion is accompanied by ritual as a means of symbolically conveying the religious message. What are the similarities between the ritual on T.V. and that commonly used in church services? What is different?

4. Sociologists focus on groups. What can you say about the audiences for a T.V. broadcast, and those for a church service? For example, are they a secondary group, a voluntary group, an open group, or a closed group? Just what are the characteristics of each audience, and how does this affect individual participants?

5. Religious norms may need some kind of sanctions to back them up. What control do the established churches have over members of their congregation? What control do T.V. evangelists have over their audiences?

6. What techniques can preachers on television use to reach and make contact with their audience?

7. What social or individual factors predispose individuals towards religion?

8. How does television evangelism (such as the three programmes cited in the article) meet these needs?

9. Does televangelism provide a solution to anomie?

10. The article states "Critics say that the program preys on (the) low-income, infirm and uneducated..." and "Burke admits that some of the program's audience may be poor and uneducated..." Do you consider this a criticism of the programme? Explain why or why not.

Intermarriages worry some Jews

Maintenance of Religious Identity

INTRODUCTION

Jews are a relatively small percentage of the Canadian population. Their long history of persecution and wide dispersion has made the Jewish people acutely sensitive to threats to maintaining their religious and cultural identity. Any decline in numbers for whatever reason is therefore threatening.

Marriage to others of the same religious and cultural background perpetuates both the religion and the community. Intermarriage with other religious groups makes the perpetuation of the Jewish religion and culture problematic, since it lessens the likelihood of Jewish beliefs being passed on to the children and their children by the normal process of socialization and through membership in a Jewish family network.

MONTREAL (CP)—As intermarriage between Jews and non-Jews in North America increases, the age-old issue of assimilation is being thrust onto centre stage in Judaism once more.

While traditionalists are becoming only too happy to welcome converts into the fold, they are worrying about cases where the non-Jewish partner does not convert and the couple gravitates away from Judaism.

As many as 40 per cent of American Jews are choosing non-Jewish partners, up sharply from about 10 per cent during the 1950s, said Dr. Larry Grossman of the American Jewish Committee.

McGill University sociologist Morton Weinfeld said intermarriage runs about 25 per cent in most of Canada, up from less than 10 per cent in the mid-sixties.

The increase has forced Jewish leadership to consider new ways to reach intermarried couples who wed in civil ceremonies and whose non-observant Jewish partners may otherwise be lost to a minority which has always feared for its survival.

Intermarriage is "one of the most sensitive questions facing the rabbinate today," said Rabbi Kenneth Segal, head rabbi at Montreal's Temple Emmau-El-Beth-Sholom.

Segal is one of a rare breed in Canada—a rabbi willing to officiate at a marriage between a Jew and a non-Jew. But he does so only on a highly-selective basis, and he will not co-officiate with Christian clergy.

Neither Orthodox nor Conservative rabbis will officiate at mixed marriges, insisting on prior conversion of the non-Jew.

Rabbi Howard Joseph, of Montreal's Spanish and Portuguese synagogue, has counselled hundreds of people considering marriage to Jews.

"About half of those who inquire don't come back because they realize it's a very serious and difficult step," he said.

Conversion entails a lengthy period of study and judgment by a board of rabbis that the would-be convert is sincere.

"Religion is not like music, where you go one week to a rock concert and the next week to classical," said Joseph. "Religion involves a commitment."

Winnipeg Free Press, Tuesday, August 7, 1984, p. 25. With permission of The Canadian Press.

Concepts to consider:

Assimilation, beliefs, commitment, conversion, family, marriage, religion, socialization.

QUESTIONS

1. What percentage of the Canadian population is Jewish?

2. What is the percentage increase in the numbers of Jews marrying non-Jews? Is this a significant increase? Can you tell from the article?

3. What factors might contribute to the rising number of Jews marrying non-Jews?

4. Define belief. Explain what is involved in religious beliefs.

5. What is involved in conversion? What psychological and social factors contribute to making converting to another religion a serious and difficult step?

6. What is meant by commitment? How can a religious commitment be fulfilled?

7. Define assimilation. Explain the connection between assimilation and Jews marrying non-Jews.

8. Why do Jews worry if some of their number marry non-Jews? What are the long-term implications?

9. Under what circumstances do people of other religious faiths worry about marriage to outsiders?

FIND A CLIPPING

Religious beliefs find a variety of expression in different cultures within a society. Each may have its own church or religious place of worship, since religion involves a community of believers.

Canada has a substantial number of immigrants who brought the religious beliefs of their homeland with them. Because many second and third-generation Canadians retain the religious beliefs of their forebears, there are a wide variety of churches and religious gatherings in most Canadian cities and towns.

Look at the religion section of your local paper (usually found in the weekend paper), identify and list all the different churches and religious meetings by church, denomination, sect, or group as appropriate. What does this tell you about the cultural composition of your city or town? Do you know where the different religious groups came from? Are there other religious groups in your locality that you know of who do not advertise in the paper? Do these religious differences lead to conflict of any sort?

17

The Economy and Work

In every society there are established, institutionalized ways of producing goods and services and of distributing them to consumers. The economy refers to that institutionalized area of social life which involves the production, distribution and consumption of goods and services.

Canada can be called a mixed capitalist economy. Goods and services are produced by privately owned firms for profit, and the profit motive provides the incentive to produce. In Canada and most western capitalist countries there is also significant government production through Crown corporations, and government intervention and regulation in the operations of the economy; for example, in government efforts to control inflation, in providing tax incentives to investment, in passing laws to protect consumers, in labour legislation.

Both the production of goods and services and their distribution are characterized by an ad-

vanced division of labour and a high level of specialization, as illustrated by the different jobs people do and by the interdependence with others which has been created by specialization.

The economy affects all our lives, occupying as it does a major portion of our time and effort, as producers or consumers. In order to live we need the basic necessities; beyond that we desire a large number of goods and services that perhaps are not essential but that have become part of an established lifestyle. Economic exchanges are normally facilitated by the use of money; we get paid for working and exchange the money for what we want.

Work is of great importance in personal life, because it provides the income and the social status by which people evaluate themselves and others, and because it takes up a major portion of our waking hours. Work gives us a sense of personal and social identity. People measure themselves in part by their degree of involvement in the producing part of society; for example, they identify themselves to others by their occupation. Being unemployed has an impact on many people beyond the loss of income: it affects their sense of belonging and of self-worth. Even though people view work as a key component in their lives, work does not always provide people with satisfaction. They work as a means to an end, not because they take great pleasure in the work itself.

The cartoon that follows makes an apt point on the intersection of the economy and family life and humorously shows the profound impact social institutions have on individuals' personal lives. The demands of the family and the economic order have to be reconciled by parents and working in the labour force frequently conflicts with duties and pleasures associated with family life.

The next article deals with a variant on the usual pattern of exchange which has arisen in response to an economic downswing and high taxation. Not all economic relationships involve monetary exchange. Barter, exchanging gifts, and redistribution have all operated in societies as a means of distributing goods, and examples of these types of exchanges can be found today in Canada. Different types of social relationships prevail where these means of exchange operate instead of interactions based on money.

The third article deals with a new approach to bargaining between labour and management. Relations between management and labour are commonly presumed to be antagonistic. Ideally, bargaining in labour disputes should aim to reduce or work around the antagonism and bring the two sides closer to identifying with the other's point of view.

Turning a Social Institution Upside Down

INTRODUCTION

Economic activities, like other aspects of social life, follow established patterns. Generally we accept routinized activities and do not question them. For example, young people looking for a job expect that the starting pay will be low and hope that the pay and their income will increase with age and experience. However, this pattern has an impact on what young people can and cannot do and on famly life when children are small.

Occasionally it is good to be provocative and ask, "What if... ?" For example, what if the established patterns of work life were changed to give high wage rates and salaries when the children in the family are young and reduced salaries as workers get older? Or suppose parents could schedule retirement for a few years when the children are born, then work until their dying day. Read the cartoon and be a little whimsical; use your imagination and consider alternatives. (Think of the alternative first and only identify the difficulties of implementing it afterwards. Remember that these difficulties are the result of constraints imposed by economic relationships. This approach is useful in identifying constraints and in seeing how they might be changed.)

Activities that are institutionalized, bounded as they are by widely held beliefs, values and norms do not change fast; thus we tend to think of them as fixed. But change can take place and can be directed if some original thinkers push hard enough in a particular direction.

Concepts to consider:

Beliefs, economy, family, norms, role, social change, social institution, values, work.

FOR BETTER OR FOR WORSE

QUESTIONS

1. Explain sociologically why the little boy's grandfather has time and money to go fishing now.

2. Why couldn't he go when his children were his grandson's age?

3. Why do wages and salaries rise as workers get older?

4. Can fathers take time off to be with children when the children are young? Why not?

5. Explore both the individual and social consequences of reversing the "normal" economic work life. Suppose wages and salaries started high and declined with age?

6. What would be the personal and social consequences of retirement with a pension for 10 years when the first child is born, followed by work until your dying day?

7. What would be the impact of wages or salaries related to family size and/or responsibilities? (The pay in the armed forces used to vary according to the number of dependents.)

8. In times of severe recession and high unemployment, the institutionalized patterns of work are disrupted. In such periods much effort by government and individuals is directed at attempting to re-establish what has been lost (e.g., full employment). Also some changes to take place that are adaptations to the new economic circumstances. What examples of these trends can you identify in the past 5 years?

An Unconventional Pattern of Distribution

INTRODUCTION

In Canada, as in other countries, money serves to buy most goods and services. Money serves to purchase necessities and all the many other consumer items and services that are difficult to do without because they are considered part of an established lifestyle. The possession of these goods and the ability to purchase the services is mark of a family's social standing.

People are forced to adapt when the maintenance of "normal" lifestyles gets expensive and taxes are felt to be too heavy. Other means of distribution may be adopted; the alternatives affect the economy, and also involve different forms of social relationships between the producer and the consumer.

This article discusses the underground economy (often called the hidden economy), that is, the economy hidden from normal financial records accessible to tax audit. Barter, as the article says, is not new, but it is enjoying renewed popularity in Canada.

Bartering making big comeback

By Richard Gwyn

If you live in Winnipeg, you can get the services of a lawyer, a chartered accountant, a plumber, a carpenter, an electrician, a mechanic and of others for free. You pay with skills or services of your own of equivalent value.

In Ottawa and Montreal, you can take your car to a co-op garage, get advice from a licenced mechanic, open up the hood, and then hope that the plug you unplug is the one you were supposed to unplug.

In Toronto, you can join Skills Exchange, a non-profit organization that offers courses by experts on subjects ranging from cooking to financial planning.

Barter has always existed and, indeed, for most of the time was the only economic activity that did exist since no one trusted the coinage, which the kings were always clipping. Today, all families do it. He humps out the garbage, she cooks. Friends and neighbors do it, without keeping a tally of who owes what to whom. Individuals barter with themselves: they decide to hammer together a backyard deck, say, rather than hire a contractor.

Barter thrives naturally in rural areas. In an Eastern Ontario hamlet, unnamed so that Revenue Canada can't pinpoint it, the farmers exchange vegetables, fruits, sides of beef, honey, jams and jellies, equipment, and arrange for the vet to nurse their animals in exchange for a winter's worth of snow-ploughing his drive and do likewise with the local dentist.

The new phenomenon is that urban middle class, to stretch its pennies further, is taking to barter.

Also new, in its extent, is the degree to which the prime motive for plunging into the "underground economy" has become to escape taxes.

By definition, the "underground economy" cannot be measured. A recent University of Alberta study guessed it at 10 – 15 per cent of the gross national product, or about $50 billion. Other estimates are much lower. Whatever its size, the underground economy today is the healthiest part, and the only growing part, of our economy.

The urge to avoid taxes scarcely is new. Officially, not a taxi driver or waiter or waitress in Canada ever is tipped. Every cleaning lady and baby sitter works for free. No garage sale ever makes any money.

In contrast to the U.S., where studies have put the tax loss as high as $120 billion, the tax leakages in Canada have been until now, tolerable. Revenue Canada audits only about one per cent of

Concepts to consider:

Barter, division of labour, dysfunction, economy, function, government, industrial society, norms of evasion, sanctions, secondary relationships, social contract, social institution, social interaction.

personal tax returns. We are one of only five countries—the U.S., Australia, Sweden, New Zealand—where citizens voluntarily fill in their returns entirely by themselves (about one in five resort to professional help).

Paying taxes amounts to a social contract, a fee paid for government services. The contract is beginning to crack apart, because more and more Canadians are dissatisfied with the services that government provides in return. "Tax cheating may become a way of life for many people," warns pollster Martin Goldfarb.

Whatever the causes, there is now a striking readiness by people to 'fess up to tax fiddles. The small businessman who says, "I'm just not going to report my (company) leased car; they haven't got enough accountants to catch me." Retailers who admit that not every receipt has been entered into the cash register. Older Canadians who confide they've helped their children with concessionary mortgage loans at 10 per cent, say, which, became paid-back in cash and so not entered as taxable income, earn them as much, net, as if invested conventionally. Investors who brag they've exchanged their mortgage interest debt, which isn't tax-deductible, into investment debt, which is.

Provided governments regain their legitimacy, a sense of civic responsibility will re-assert itself.

Barter itself, though, is integral to the new ethic of frugality. As it takes hold, the changes in social attitudes could be far-reaching.

"Less and less is socio-economic status going to be determined by what you have," says Goldfart. "More and more it will be determined by what you can do, from carpentry to composing poetry."

Jim Cook, a chartered accountant, started Bartermart in Winnipeg last January. "The key is the computer system," he explains. A plumber, say, does $200 worth of work for a lawyer. Among the club's members—a probable 1,000 by the year's end—the plumber now has 200 credit points which he can claim against anyone, and the lawyer will have 200 debits, which anyone can claim.

"Everyone has surplus time or skills," says Cook. "Barter just allows them to swap among each other to best effect." He himself hopes to barter the part-time use of his canoe for some work in his backyard. (Bartermart records, by the way, are all available for inspection by Revenue Canada.)

The Citizen, Ottawa, Monday, June 7, 1982, p. 37.

QUESTIONS

1. Explain what is meant by barter.

2. What is the difference between barter and what is normatively defined as the way to obtain goods and services in Canada?

3. Why isn't barter normally widely used?

4. Under what conditions can barter take place today in Canada?

5. How is barter being facilitated as described in this article?

6. What is meant by a social contract? What is the example given in the article?

7. Why do people accept that they should pay taxes to the government?

8. Why do people avoid taxes? Is this an example of norms of evasion? Explain.

9. Is the underground economy functional or dysfunctional for the social system? Explain your answer and identify ways in which it is either or both.

A New Style in Labour Negotiations

INTRODUCTION

Unions serve to mitigate the harsh effects of the economic system through negotiations over wages, working conditions and fringe benefits, and by securing protection against arbitrary dismissal and other arbitrary acts of management. Even in hard times, unions can mitigate the effect of layoffs and shutdowns in the interests of their members.

Approximately one-third of the Canadian labour force is unionized. Workers who are individually powerless in negotiations with management can achieve a stronger bargaining position by organizing to bargain collectively with individual employers or industry-wide employers' associations. Once workers have won the right to form unions, management has to negotiate with them. Differences are usually settled by discussion. In the less common but more widely publicized situations in which the two sides cannot agree, strikes and lockouts may take place.

This article from the The Financial Post, a business newspaper, deals with the proposal to change the provincial labour laws in Manitoba. The change would introduce a new means of settling disputes when negotiations are not resolving the differences between employers and workers.

NDP plays baseball card to curb labor disputes

By Edward Greenspon

WINNIPEG—The Manitoba government plans to give protagonists in labor disputes the option of submitting to a rarely used form of arbitration instead of resorting to strikes and lockouts.

Under a procedure known as Final Offer Selection (FOS), both a union and management would submit offers on unresolved items to an impartial selector, who would include one package or the other in the collective agreement. The selector could not decide on a combination of the two proposals.

Any strikes or lockouts in progress would end as soon as the FOS option was chosen.

"I think we've matured enough that an alternative to work stoppage is timely," says Mary Beth Dolin, Manitoba's Labor minister.

The FOS method is best known for its use in professional baseball salary arbitrations. It is not common in Canadian collective bargaining and is not included in any provincial labor legislation.

Advocates say it forces both parties to make reasonable offers because the proposal judged best by the selector is accepted in full. But critics say this may force the selector into accepting weak solutions rather than working toward a stronger compromise and may leave the losing party feeling embittered.

The FOS proposal is the centrepiece of the New Democratic government's white paper on changes to Manitoba's labor laws. Legislation is expected to be introduced in early June, the first significant amendments to the province's Labor Relations Act in 12 years.

Although uncommon in this country, final offer selection can be used at present with the consent of both management and labor. It has been used in settling contracts at the University of Manitoba.

The Manitoba government's suggested approach is novel, however, in that either management or a union could request that a dispute be resolved by FOS. The request could be made at any time during negotiations.

But workers would have to approve the request before a selector is appointed, an aspect of the Manitoba proposal that irritates business.

David Newman, a prominent

management lawyer in Winnipeg, says unions are being given a veto over FOS that is not available to employers, giving labor a new tool to supplement traditional strike action rather than substituting for it.

"It can be used by the union to prevent or end a lockout. But it can't be used by an employer to end a strike unless the employees support it," he says. "And therefore when a union is winning a strike it is unlikely to be used, whereas when the union is losing a strike it is likely to be used."

The government emphasizes that its proposal does not eliminate the right of unions to strike and the proposal has won the support of the Manitoba Federation of Labor. But the Winnipeg Chamber of Commerce and the Manitoba Fashion Institute both have come out against the FOS plan.

Dolin says business critics are failing to note the difference between the members of the bargaining unit, who can veto the FOS process, and the union, which has just the same right to request the process as management.

"In the case of a work stoppage," she says of conversations she has held with business leaders, "the employers have maintained that the employees really don't want to be out on strike, but that they've been talked into it by the big union types. This is their chance to prove that.

"What we are saying is that both the bargaining agent and the employer have the opportunity to go to the workers and to say: 'Do you want a work stoppage to gamble on getting what you want in a contract or do you want to stay on the job and try to write the best contract possible and submit it to a final selector?'"

Gary Doer, president of the Manitoba government Employees Association, likes the FOS idea and says it will be better for both labor and business in the long run because it will foster labor stability.

"In the shorter run, if you have the hammer—and business has the hammer now—it hurts them. Later on, when labor has the hammer, it will take away the ability to bluff bargain."

But Keith Godden, president of the Winnipeg Chamber of Commerce, says Manitoba already has an enviable labor record and so there is no reason to introduce an innovation like FOS. "If it's not bust, don't fix it," he says.

There are other concerns about final offer selection besides who will benefit most from it. Collective agreements tend to be complex documents with a number of unrelated clauses. A selector could easily be faced with a proposal in which six out of 10 clauses are superior while the other four are inferior.

'One option'

For that reason, final offer selection is best suited to single issues, such as whether a baseball player should be paid $200,000 a year or $300,000, says Don Carter, a law professor at Queen's University, Kingston, Ont., and a former chairman of the Ontario Labor Relations Board. In more complicated agreements, it is difficult to weigh all the factors and come down on just one side or the other.

"It is one option," Carter says. "The great mistake is to regard it as a panacea."

But Dolin says that experience with FOS in other countries shows that only a small number of the items in a collective agreement actually go to the selector. Most issues are settled beforehand, she says, and unions and management can still reach a negotiated agreement right up to the time the selector makes his ruling.

The Financial Post, June 2, 1984, p. 8. With permission of The Financial Post.

Concepts to consider:

Arbitration, capitalism, conciliation, conflict, co-operation, formal organization, goals, labour relations, law, negotiation, power, profit.

QUESTIONS

1. Is conflict inherent in labour/management relations?

2. What theoretical perspective deals with management-union relations most effectively?

3. What power do workers have in disputes with management?

4. What power do employers have in labour disputes with employees?

5. Explain Final Offer Selection briefly.

6. What are the alternative methods of settling labour disputes?

7. What are the advantages of final offer selection compared with alternative methods of settling labour disputes?

8. What are the disadvantages?

9. Why are employers likely to be against Final Offer Selection?

FIND A CLIPPING

Alienation describes the feelings of powerlessness, helplessness and isolation that people experience when they are in situations they cannot control. Conditions of work are often described as alienating in modern society. Workers may experience similar feelings when they are unemployed. Find an article that illustrates alienation in a work-related situation, or an article that describes the feelings of unemployed workers. Explain your understanding of the situation described in the article and the social and economic causes of alienation.

18

The State of Politics

The established political system in any country provides legitimate ways through which some individuals and groups gain the right to make decisions in the general interests of the electorate and enforce those decisions. The exercise of power has to have backing, with force if necessary. The state, according to Max Weber (1946) is the institution that successfully claims the monopoly on the right to use force within a given territory. In Canada, only the police and the armed forces have the legal right to coerce people. Both are under state control.

Government refers to the political party that has been elected to exercise the power of the state at any given time. Canada has a representative democracy, which means those exercising power can be held accountable by the electorate and the party forming the government can be changed peacefully, under specified conditions. Democratic processes are accepted in Canada, as in many other countries, as the appropriate and legitimate way of changing the government.

The right to participate in the political process and the ways to do so are also institutionalized. The right to participation is limited to some degree in Canada (though rights are not denied to the extent that they are elsewhere in the world). It is important to understand the ways in which the right to vote, to work for a political party, and freedom to express opinions can be safeguarded and perpetuated. The first two articles in this section examine voting and other issues relating to participation in the political process.

In Canada the federal government is responsible for all matters of national interest such as defence, the maintenance of social order within the country, taxation, inter-provincial trade, and major transportation routes. Provincial governments (sub-central governments) are responsible for matters that were originally contained within provincial boundaries, such as health, education, social services, control over resources, and promoting development of the provincial economy. The term political economy refers to the interconnections between the economy and political institutions. The links between the two are extensive. The federal and provincial governments can have considerable impact on the economy, and hence on people's daily lives through the laws passed, including taxation and other fiscal measures. The third article in this section examines one example of the business relationship between the government of Saskatchewan and business within that province. The extent and ways in which the government should be involved are ideological issues and vary depending on which political party is elected to form the government.

The power to control others may be based on force; others can then be coerced into obedience. Power that is regarded as legitimate by those who submit to it is labelled authority. Authority may have its basis of legitimacy in tradition (traditional authority); in impersonal norms and laws where the position of the person gives them the right to exercise authority over others (legal-rational authority); or in the personality of the leader (charismatic authority) (Weber, 1946).

Power and authority should be distinguished from influence, which refers to the ability to sway people's actions or opinions but which has no sanctions to back it.

Maintaining Democracy

INTRODUCTION

This article in the Telegraph-Journal provides information about the registration of voters and voting prior to the federal election on September 4, 1984. Similar information and announcements of the dates appeared in newspapers across the country, as happens before every federal election.

Democracy is institutionalized in Canadian society, and most citizens have the right to vote. However, in Canada, in the past and at present, certain groups are excluded from voting. The criteria for eligibility vary depending on whether it is a federal, provincial or municipal election. In answering the questions that follow, consider what the implications are of setting criteria for deciding who can vote.

In order to cast their vote, potential voters must be on the voters' list. Assess the effectiveness of the method of enumeration in ensuring that the maximum possible number of voters are actually registered to vote. The media have a role to play in informing the potential electorate of their rights, thereby encouraging them to get on the voters' list.

Enumeration begins today

OTTAWA (CP)—Urban and rural enumerators in Canada's 282 federal ridings begin knocking on doors today to compile lists of eligible voters for the September 4 federal election.

The 110,000 enumerators will spend seven days, including Sunday, tracking down the estimated 16.5 million Canadian citizens who are 18 years or older and eligible to vote.

They will visit every home in their riding, at least once during the week, and twice if necessary. If both visits are unsuccessful, they will leave a notice asking residents to register by contacting the returning officer in their riding as soon as possible.

Preliminary list

Although urban residents have until August 17 to register, Elections Canada urge them to get their names on the preliminary voters' list before August 7 because numbers on the preliminary list will be used to determine election spending limits for candidates and political parties.

Urban residents who do not have their names on final voters' lists by August 17 will lose their right to vote in this election. Rural voters may be sworn-in election day if they are accompanied by someone from their polling district who can vouch for them.

City dwellers who will be away from their homes from Friday until August 17 may register with the Elections Canada office in their constituency before they leave or ask a neighbor to give their names to enumerators.

Because of privacy concerns, voters' lists are no longer posted on street corners nor sent to every household. Instead, registered voters will receive notices in the mail advising them that their names have been recorded.

Amendments to the preliminary lists begin August 3 as revising agents or special enumerators try to contact urban and rural residents missed by regular enumerators.

They will submit the names they collect to the revision court, which sits August 15, 16 and 17. Revision officers will add names to the final voters' list when the court sitting ends.

Voters who were excluded from the preliminary lists and not visited by revising agents may appear before the revision court themselves to have their names added to the final list.

Registered voters who will be away from home September 4

Concepts to consider:

Coercion, democracy, law, majority group, mass media, minority group, power, rights, social inequality, vote.

may cast their ballots at advance polls August 25, 27 and 28 or at the office of the riding's returning officer after August 12.

Elderly, infirm and pregnant voters are urged to make use of advance polls, which will open at noon and close at 8 p.m.

Last resort

Voting is permitted at the office of the returning officer as a last resort. Those who wish to do so will be required to swear a declaration that they will be away from home for the advance polls and for election day.

The returning officer will accommodate voters from 12 p.m. to 6 p.m. and from 7 p.m. to 9 p.m. every day except Sunday from August 13 to 24 and again from August 29 to 31. Only registered voters may vote before election day.

Voters are required to cast their ballots in the polling district where they usually live and not in districts where they have summer homes.

On election day, polls will be open from 9 a.m. to 8 p.m. local time.

The Telegraph-Journal, Saint John, Friday, July 27, 1984, p. 3. With permission of The Canadian Press.

QUESTIONS

1. Explain what is meant by democracy.

2. How is it decided who can have the vote?

3. What are the necessary qualifications to be an "eligible voter" in federal elections in Canada?

4. What are the implications of certain groups being excluded from the list of eligible voters?

5. What is the goal of enumeration? How do the methods cited in the article assist in achieving this goal? What difficulties are avoided? What problems remain?

6. What steps are taken to ensure that everyone who wants to vote can actually cast a vote?

7. Does having the vote ensure fair treatment for minority groups? Explain your answer.

8. What is expected of you in your role of voter?

9. Would it matter to you personally if you did not have the right to vote in a Canadian federal election? Explain your concern or lack of it. If you do not have the right to vote does it bother you? Why or why not?

10. How important and effective is the role of the media in informing potential voters of the means of getting registered? How else would they know?

Government examines its own discrimination

Under What Circumstances Should Political Rights Be Denied?

INTRODUCTION

Civil servants are appointed to work in the administration putting laws and regulations into practice after they are passed, investigating the need for changes in laws, and in policy decision making. Their position requires a clear understanding of the workings of government and in many cases gives them access to much sensitive information on possible future government programmes and policies.

With the exception of a few very senior positions which may change when the government changes, employment in the civil services is considered a continuing career, and civil servants are presumed to serve successive governments of various political persuasions without bias or favour.

In reading the editorial from The Guardian, reflect on the implications of the various laws under debate. Canadians generally believe in their right to participate in the political process, yet some people are barred from doing so. Exclusions need to be justified.

Under Prince Edward Island provincial law, the Civil Services Act, civil servants have not been allowed to join a political party, to attend political meetings or to run as candidates. The Federal Charter of Rights and

It's a Dark Ages proposition that government employees are prohibited by legislation from actively participating in political matters. The only redeeming aspect of the situation is that they are allowed to vote.

Governments, of course, have their reasons for imposing such restrictions—civil servants can't join a political party, can't attend political meetings, can't offer as a candidate at election time.

But now, in this province at least, it looks as though there is some light at the end of the tunnel. The minister responsible for the Civil Service Act, Albert Fogarty, has said the government is now considering the issue of political rights for its employees. Hopefully, that means that the rights taken away by legislation will be returned.

Meanwhile, the president of the Union of Public Sector Employees, Sandy MacKay, anticipates some changes in the situation when the Charter of Rights and Freedoms comes into effect next year. As he sees it, the charter's right to the freedom of belief and association will force the province to change its restrictive legislation. But it must be remembered that legislatures have the power to nullify or revoke through legislation provisions of the charter for five-year periods, apparently forever.

Be that as it may, there seems to be some support within government for returning political rights in some measure to its employees. At least, one could take that interpretation from Mr. Fogarty's remarks when he said "...the principle involved is clearly pretty simple... it's a matter of deciding if some members of the civil service should be given political rights and I don't think cabinet will have any problem making a decision on this."

Freedoms may prevent such discrimination, although the provinces do have the option of opting out of the provisions of the Charter. This editorial argues that a group previously excluded from political participation should now be included. Discrimination may be justified in some circumstances, but consider what the criteria should be.

Concepts to consider:

Beliefs, democracy, discrimination, government, law, norms, politics, rights, role, values.

Nevertheless, it never pays to try to second-guess a cabinet minister. For, what is the principle that is clearly pretty simple? Is it that public employees must be discriminated against and not allowed to enjoy the democratic political rights possessed by the rest of society as government, with its penchant for secrecy, may fear that some embarrassing information may get out at electioneering time to the public that pays the bills? Or is it that members of the public service are not second-class citizens and are morally, if not now legally, entitled to enjoy the same rights as anyone else?

The latter is the preferable principle, by far.

An enlightened government will subscribe to it.

The Guardian, Charlottetown, Friday, November 9, 1984, p. 4.

QUESTIONS

1. What is the role of "civil servant"?

2. What reasons could lie behind the Prince Edward Island law which excludes civil servants from joining a political party, attending political meetings, or running as candidates in an election?

3. Explain discrimination. Can the law preventing the activities listed in question (2) be called discriminatory if reasons are given for the banning?

4. What reasons can you give for allowing civil servants to participate fully in all political activities?

5. Would changing the law make any difference to civil servants' political beliefs? Are their political beliefs likely to influence their actions? Explain.

6. What might changing the law do to the public image of civil servants.

7. The Charter of Rights and Freedoms guarantees freedom of belief and association. To what activities do these refer?

8. What are political rights? How can political rights be safeguarded?

9. Should political rights ever be limited? Consider other groups besides civil servants.

Interaction Between the Government and the Economy

INTRODUCTION

The provincial governments in Canada can have considerable influence on the economy within provincial boundaries. The federal government's economic policies can also have a significant impact. Successful provincial government economic measures can prolong the tenure of the government by ensuring their re-election because voters benefit from the employment and prosperity. How government goes about promoting economic prosperity depends in large part on the ideology of the party in power. Individual business executives make decisions for their own companies but these decisions are often influenced by provincial and federal government economic policies. The Saskatchewan government in 1984, headed by Premier Grant Devine, was Conservative.

Find out more about Saskatchewan Business Incentive Programs

The 1984 provincial budget contained a number of measures designed to assist Saskatchewan business. Saskatchewan Tourism and Small Business and the Melville Chamber of Commerce are sponsoring an information meeting to provide full details on four business-related programs:

- Venture Capital Program

- Fixed Rate Financing

- Industrial Incentive Program

- Tax Reduction for Manufacturers and Processors

Representatives of Saskatchewan Tourism and Small Business, Saskatchewan Economic Development and Trade, Saskatchewan Finance and the Saskatchewan Securities Commission will be in attendance to answer your questions.

This important meeting will be held June 11 at 7 p.m. in the Prince William Motor Inn.

It's an opportunity to find out how these programs can benefit business in Saskatchewan. If you plan to attend, please call the Melville Chamber of Commerce, or the regional office of Tourism and Small Business.

Putting our faith in the future to work at building today.

—Saskatchewan Tourism and Small Business, Hon. Jack Klein, Minister.

The Four-Town Journal, Wednesday, June 6, 1984, p. 14.

Concepts to consider:

Capitalism, economy, government, ideology, influence, political economy, regionalism, socialism.

QUESTIONS

1. Define government. What is the role of government?

2. What is meant by political economy?

3. In what ways can the government influence the economy?

4. Explain what is meant by ideology.

5. Would ideological considerations influence government actions? Explain.

6. Why would the Saskatchewan government want to influence the economy?

7. What impacts could the measures mentioned in the advertisement have if successful? What effects could they have if unsuccessful?

8. What theoretical perspective would you use to explain government actions in the business field?

9. What is the role of the media in the relations between the government and the economy?

FIND A CLIPPING

Find an article in a newspaper or magazine illustrating the exercise of authority over others: an incident involving the police, a legal judgment, a decision by a regulatory agency, the actions of immigration officials, a new municipal by-law, the duties of a security guard, or a decision of a federal government official or of a cabinet minister.

Define authority and discuss the following points: Explain the situation in the article that you found, and discuss how the authority is exercised in this situation. What is the basis on which the authority is regarded as legitimate—is it tradition, legal-rational, or charisma? Explain exactly why people obey, or the consequences if they rebel. How can the authority be enforced? What sanctions exist to back it up? Explain your answers, giving illustrations from the clipping as well as using your own knowledge.

19

Urbanization

Sociologists are interested in studying the patterns of social life in communities of differing size. Urbanization refers to the movement of people into settlements that are large, densely populated and more heterogeneous than rural areas. The trend in Canada and elsewhere has been towards urbanization.

Canada is now one of the most urbanized countries in the world. Three-quarters of the Canadian population lives in urban centres. The Canadian census defines the urban population as persons living in an area having a population concentration of 1000 or more and a population density of 400 or more per square kilometre (1981 Census). Cities and the continuous built-up areas around them are labelled "Census Metropolitan Areas" and have a population of 100,000 or more. Toronto, Hamilton, Vancouver, Montreal, Winnipeg, Calgary, Halifax, and Kitchener are examples.

The large-scale urbanization with which we are familiar depends on industrialization. Our way of life depends on advanced scientific knowledge and on its technological applications. Knowledge of the means of growing large volumes of food and of food preservation is what makes large concentrations of population possible. Cities and towns depend on highly developed transportation systems to bring in food and other supplies.

Many sociologists believe that the concentration of people into cities and towns leads to a different lifestyle and a differing set of social values and attitudes from those prevailing in rural areas. For example, people in cities and towns need to keep a degree of social distance from others in order to preserve some privacy and independence in their lives. They also come to depend to a great extent on publicly provided services in times of need rather than on the support of family and neighbours. Other government-provided services enhance the urban standard of living, and the demand for these services filters out to rural areas. Canadians have come to expect clean water, reliable sources of power, modern spacious housing, central heating, health services, roads and automobiles.

Urban living results in the concentration of decision making power, there being more urban constituencies than rural ones represented in provincial and federal governments. It can be argued that urbanization colours political thinking and leads to less regard for the wishes of rural inhabitants. The first article in this section protests this attitude and the lack of services in rural areas.

Growth was originally uncontrolled in most cities, but city and suburban growth is now planned. Planning involves a number of different groups in decision making on the development of sites in urban areas. The second selection in this section, a letter to the editor, relates to development in a suburban area of Victoria, B.C. The invention of the automobile and the beginning of public transport led to the growth of the "bedroom suburb,": people living on the edge of the city and working downtown. Some surburban areas have an economic base, and residents live and work in the area. As a suburban area grows more jobs are created in, for example, local shopping centres, small service industries catering to residents, gas stations, local hospitals, and nursing homes.

The final advertisement in this section deals with electric power and the attempt by the Newfoundland Light and Power Co. to educate the public in order to gain their co-operation. Canadians value a high standard of living, measured in terms of material goods and services available, and opportunities to try new things. Our values are backed by our belief that technology can dominate the environment. Occasionally, this belief is challenged.

Impact of the Metropolis on the Hinterland

INTRODUCTION

The writer of this article is supposedly expressing some of the exasperation felt by rural residents with the influence exerted from metropolitan areas. Decisions made in the urban areas have an impact on the economic development and the level of public services in rural areas. Rural residents often feel that they do not have much input into decision making.

The article is deliberately provocative. As you think about the example cited by Fred McGuinness, consider who in the political system is responsible for decision making and the ways in which services are provided to residents in rural areas.

Neighborly news

By Fred McGuinness

(McGuinness is a lecturer in Journalism at Brandon University, and columnist to *The Weekly Press*.)

I should call this the Confessions of a Paranoid.

Each week I read the weeklies and collect more stories that distress me.

The worst type deals with Them and Us.

Them are the big-city types. Most provincial laws are written on their behalf. Because legislators convene in cities and most civil servants live there, the regulations usually pay scant heed to life in the boonies. That's where Us lives.

I thought of Us this morning when I read the <u>Humboldt Journal</u>.

In part, an editorial reads, "In a rural community, we have one strike against us already just being rural as most everything is geared for the city way of life."

The <u>Dauphin Herald</u> gives me bakery food for thought. A bakeshop in that area was convicted on charges to do with labelling the products. Here's a case where the bureaucracy went mad.

In one example given, the baker sells 300 per year of a certain item. To buy pre-printed bags and keep the law-makers happy, the minimum order is for 10,000 bags. To comply with the rules, the baker must buy 30 year's supply in advance.

Says the <u>Herald</u>, "...unless government regulations pay heed to the problems faced by small-scale enterprises, those regulations could be fatal to these enterprises." Hear, hear.

A month ago I was at a day-long meeting of mayors who gathered to talk about community improvement. Several of them the week previous had been at a province-run seminar on industrial development.

The civil servants running it geared it for enterprises with start-up values of $1 million or more. The mayors checked out at noon; it wasn't for them.

Central to most rural problems is public service. The cities have 'em, the boonies don't.

You get the drift from a letter in the <u>Oxbow Herald</u>. It's a community farewell from a pair of trained ambulance attendants. They state it's not reasonable to expect them to sit by that telephone, 24 hours a day, 30 days a month. In this case the service will revert to volunteers.

At Charesholm, there's a problem finding an equitable formula for ambulance costs. Three jurisdictions now share this service. If no agreement can be reached, the largest partner will take over the service and the smaller partners will fend for themselves. A political squabble is of little interest to a farm family that needs an ambulance now, now, now.

Concepts to consider:

Census metropolitan area, city, government, ideology, influence, law, mass media, metropolitan-hinterland, politics, power, rural, urban.

The Charesholm Local Press says if a town resident has an accident or heart attack just outside the town limits, they'd better be prepared to crawl back over that boundary.

As I tot up my collection of injustices, I wonder who will solve these problems. It's tempting to look to the members of the legislature but some times I fear they forget their constituents.

Nor am I alone in my worries over rural society. The <u>Hanna Herald</u> says provincial governments pump money into transportation culture and recreational services for the city folk. The result is that the cities, "get larger, dirtier, and more uncomfortable."

And just as I'm going to press, I learn about the citizens in the Nipawin district who had their signals from a community-owned dish cut off, orders of the C.R.T.C.

Last time I was in Toronto, I counted 58 T.V. signals in their listings. In some parts of the prairies where no cable is available, you're restricted to CBC and CTV.

I say that's 58 for Them, and two for Us.

The Potashville Miner-Journal, Esterhazy, Saskatchewan, Wednesday, June 6, 1984, p. 4.

QUESTIONS

1. What is the definition of rural used by Statistics Canada in the census?

2. Explain what is meant by referring to an area as "the boonies." Is the term derogatory? What is implied about living in a city compared with rural living?

3. Give an example of a government regulation that works in an urban area but not in a rural area. Use the article or an example of your own.

4. Is it likely to be true that "most provincial laws are written (for) the big-city types"? Explain why you answer as you do.

5. Give an example of a public service offered in the city that may be lacking in rural areas. Why is it not provided in rural areas?

6. Could services be organized differently to ensure that they are provided in rural areas?

7. Why are rural inhabitants likely to want the same services, business incentives, and recreational and cultural services as city folk?

8. What theory would you consider appropriate for analysing the relations between the "census metropolitan areas" and rural areas?

9. How would you assess "Neighborly News" as a piece of newspaper writing?

Input into the Urban Planning Process

INTRODUCTION

The intersection of Cadboro Bay Road and Foul Bay Road is a major intersection in Victoria, B.C. Foul Bay Road is also the boundary between the City of Victoria and the separate municipality of Oak Bay, a middle-class/upper-middle-class residential suburb. The intersection has a shopping centre on one corner dominated by a Safeway store, with other retail outlets and a liquor store. Two sites are under debate; one corner which is the subject of this letter was vacated by an automobile dealership, leaving a large parcel of land available for development. Reference is made in the letter to Oak Bay's other shopping areas; the largest is known as The Village, and there are two other smaller centres.

Although this letter deals with a very specific development, the situation is a recurring one in cities and towns across Canada as land becomes available for redevelopment in districts that are already established. The process of urban development and renewal is now controlled by zoning, and locally elected councils are faced with making decisions as to the use to which the land should and should not be put. The process of decision making is bureaucratic in nature. There are ways in which the various groups affected can contribute to the decision making process. Some groups will be more effective than others in exerting influence on the decision makers. The press plays a role by informing the public in reports, in editorial comment, and in providing a forum where citizens can comment on the process via letters to the editor. The decision is important because the development will affect the neighbourhood for many decades to come.

Letters
Not impressed
with report

Letter by Helen Slade

(A critique of the report submitted by the Eikos Group—"Land Use Study—Intersection of Cadboro Bay Road and Foul Bay Road.")

In part three of the report on page three the planner Dan Janczewski states that, "As the primary writer of the community plan, I can confidently state that the intention was to retain these specific sites for commercial purposes."

But nowhere in this report does he distinguish between the different types of commercial zoning. Commercial auto zoning and commercial retail zoning are quite different. They generate different types and amounts of vehicular and pedestrian traffic which subsequently impacts upon adjoining and nearby residential areas.

On page four of the report Paul Rollo's study has concluded that "the impact of a commercial/retail type of development at these sites upon other existing business areas, such as the Village, would be diminished."

As a resident and someone who shops in Oak Bay, I have to disagree. I believe that a commercial/retail development on the site in question would definitely have impact on other commercial/retail areas in Oak Bay, specifically, the Village, Foul Bay/Allenby, and Estevan. Because there is a shopping area on the Victoria side of this intersection, another one on this site would reinforce the loca-

tion convenience for shoppers using the Safeway and accompanying stores.

Paragraph E states that the use of subject sites would likely be for "a financial institution, food store, insurance/real estate, specialty food store, restaurant or similar."

These facilities already exist at this intersection or close by. Consequently, somebody's business trade would suffer.

On page six, the section dealing with traffic, says that "The possible use of this site for a new commercial or apartment development is not expected to raise traffic levels to the point which was experienced when the car dealership was in operation."

I disagree with this statement. It is obvious that the type of vehicular traffic associated with a commercial/retail area—customers, delivery trucks, garbage trucks, etc.—is much heavier than the traffic which used the Datsun centre.

The other point that is overlooked by the planner is that if both sites in question are developed as commercial/retail shopping areas, then together with the traffic using the Safeway shopping area, we would have a very heavily-used intersection at Foul Bay and Cadboro Bay.

On page seven, the planner talks about suitable development

of the southern site. What he fails to say is that this site has been rezoned by a previous council to retail zone E-general use. While council may or may not regret having made that decision—it stands.

On page eight the planner says that this area is an important entrance to Oak Bay and "Prior to council approving any form of development, objectives should be established for two subject sites, including such items as:

Lighting; signage; building character; landscaping; relationships to the street; relationship to adjacent structures; and provision of design features.

Yes, I agree.

Over two years ago when I gave my critique of the official community plan I asked that an urban design policy be included in the plan as a framework of reference. I spoke to Janczewski at the time about the value of such an urban design policy in the community plan and he said that he did not believe it was necessary.

He was wrong. Now he tells us that design objectives should be established.

Under the heading "Neighbourhood Impact" the planner says that "the reduction of impacts caused by any form of development on the surrounding neighbourboods or buildings should be a primary consideration."

Concepts
to consider:

Authority, bureaucracy, capitalism, decision making, democracy, influence, interest group, mass media, politics, power, rationalization, urbanization.

What he doesn't say and what I have already said is that with two more commercial/retail developments at this intersection we would have a heavily-used intersection. This would, of course, have an impact on nearby residential neighbourhoods.

In the final paragraph on page eight the planner contradicts himself. Having already said that he supports the retention of all commercially zoned areas, he then says he would support the extension of additional subsidized seniors housing on the south site but fails to mention that the site has already been rezoned for commercial use.

Council allocated $3,500 of taxpayers' money to pay for the planning study of this site. I am not impressed with it. I wondered at the time if it would tell council anything it didn't already know.

Oak Bay Star, Oak Bay, B.C., July 4, 1984, p. 6.

QUESTIONS

1. Why is zoning necesary in urban areas? Who makes the final decision on zoning and on whether a particular development is to be allowed?

2. How do local council members get their position?

3. What is the role of "the expert" in city planning decision making? Who is "the expert" in the situation discussed in the letter?

4. What groups of people are likely to be affected by the decision that is made on use of the corner? How is each affected?

5. Which groups are likely to make representations to the zoning board or the municipal council? Who is unlikely to be represented?

6. How much power/influence is each group likely to have over the decision makers and how can they exercise that power or influence?

7. What is the role of the media (newspapers, T.V., radio) in disseminating information to the public? What is likely to influence the role the media play?

8. What can sociologists contribute to considerations on urban development and urban planning?

9. In your opinion what criteria should be used in deciding the zoning for a land area? Explain.

Interdependencies in Modern Living

INTRODUCTION

Daily living links us with many large formal organizations whose task it is to provide services that considerably enhance modern living standards. A dependency is created on the services provided by these organizations. In a modern industrialized technological society, living standards are highly dependent on electricity supplied by large companies either privately or publicly owned. The technical expertise rests with the company, not the consumers, yet to some extent the company does need consumers' co-operation, as this advertisement indicates. To gain consumers' co-operation, the utility company has to provide them with some information as to how and under what conditions the electricity can be supplied.

Urbanization is made possible by technological advance. In turn, urbanization makes the provision of services economic because of the concentration of population. Many of these services are subsequently extended to those in rural areas, but supplying these outlying areas is more difficult. In Newfoundland and other similar areas, weather conditions can seriously affect the operations of the company.

What to do if the lights go out

Our job is to provide you with reliable continuous electric service. Despite all our efforts, power interruptions can occur, caused by lightning, high winds or ice build up on our lines. You can help us restore service as quickly as possible by knowing what to do during an interruption.

CHECK WITH YOUR NEIGHBOURS

Check your neighbours on both sides and across the street to see if they still have power. If they do, or if you still have power in some parts of your home, you may have a blown fuse or tripped circuit breaker.

TURN OFF APPLIANCES AND HEATING SYSTEM

You can help us by turning off heating equipment, ranges, pumps, water heaters and other appliances. When electric service is restored after an interruption a higher than normal load is experienced as all the lighting, heating and appliance loads of all customers affected by the interruption come on together. In cold weather this abnormal load could result in further interruptions due to overloading the lines.

Be selective in switching on electrical equipment and turn it on gradually so you won't overload the lines. Leave a light switched on, so you'll know when the power is restored.

REPORT THE TROUBLE

Report the outage to our nearest office and give your name, address and location. If the outage is widespread, our phone lines will be busy, so please try again. Once notified, we will be working to restore your service as quickly as possible. Please don't tie up phone lines by checking with us too often. But, if you see that lights are back on in your neighbourhood and if you are still without power, call us again. If you see a power line on the ground, call us immediately. Stay clear of fallen wires and avoid stepping in puddles where wires are down.

BE PREPARED

Be sure you know where the electric service pancl for your home is located. Have extra fuses available and know how to replace them.

Keep on hand – a working flashlight, matches, candles, candle holders and a battery-powered radio. As well, keep a camp stove with a supply of fuel handy. If you have a fireplace, it would be wise to have a supply of wood or coal on hand.

FREE BOOKLET

FOR MORE INFORMATION ON HOW TO HANDLE A POWER INTERRUPTION PICK UP A COPY OF THE BOOKLET 'WHAT TO DO IF THE LIGHTS GO OUT' AT ANY OF OUR OFFICES. IF YOU CAN'T GET TO ONE OF OUR OFFICES FILL OUT AND RETURN THIS COUPON AND WE WILL SEND YOU A COPY.

PLEASE SEND ME A COPY OF "WHAT TO DO IF THE LIGHTS GO OUT".

NAME_____

ADDRESS_____

TOWN_____

POSTAL
CODE_____

MAIL TO ENERGY COMMUNICATIONS
NEWFOUNDLAND LIGHT & POWER CO. LIMITED
P.O. BOX 8910
ST. JOHN'S, NFLD. A1B 3P6

NEWFOUNDLAND
LIGHT & POWER CO. LIMITED

The Evening Telegram, St. John's, Saturday, November 10, 1984, p. 7.

Concepts
to consider:

Communications,
co-operation, formal
organization,
industrialization, mass
media, modernization,
standard of living,
technology, values.

QUESTIONS

1. What causes electric power interruptions? Can these be controlled?

2. This advertisement encourages electricity consumers to co-operate with the company. Why is this exhortation necessary?

3. If the electricity supply is as unreliable as this advertisement implies, why do people buy electricity?

4. What instructions for self-sufficiency are contained in this advertisement? Why is it necessary to tell residents how to be self-sufficient?

5. Could you live without electricity permanently? What would it do to your relations with others? Be imaginative!

6. What communications channels are used, mentioned, and implied in this article? What other means of communication are there in Canadian society?

7. Is it possible to be completely self-sufficient?

FIND A CLIPPING

How does life in an urban community differ from that in a small rural community? Are there many differences?

Find a clipping that relates to, or describes, life in the city, or a remote or rural area. Read your textbook or lecture notes and discuss one of the writers who studied urbanism, or who contrasted urban and rural life. (For example, Tonnies distinguished two types of social groups, Gemeinschaft and Gesellschaft;

Louis Wirth described the characteristics of urbanism as a way of life; Herbert Gans talked of the urban villagers.)

Choose just one writer's ideas. Do these ideas appear to fit the situation in the article you have chosen? Explain what you think about the situation in the article you have found and how sociological thinking applies to it and extends our understanding.

20

Collective Behaviour, Social Movements

Sociologists are interested in groups and the ways in which people's behaviour is oriented by being part of a group. Behaviour towards others is usually guided by the shared social norms that cover the situation in which individuals find themselves. But there are, as is obvious to any observer of human behaviour, some instances where people behave collectively in ways that are not predicted but are a mass emotional reaction to the moment.

Collective behaviour refers to the behaviour of a large number of people when they act in ways which are spontaneous and unpredictable. The concept conveys the idea of people's behaviour being influenced by others around them. Collective behaviour is not necessarily dangerous. A crowd having a good time is not usually threatening; a riot where an angry mob of people is on the rampage is extremely threatening to outsiders, and difficult, if not impossible to control.

Some instances of collective behaviour come about when large numbers of people do not accept some of the prevailing values or norms, or reject the leadership or direction in the society or group. Alternative norms may emerge spontaneously from the actions of the collectivity to replace those rejected. The behaviour is "disorderly" in that it goes against the established social order accepted by most people.

Social movements are aimed at change, or at resisting social change. Social movements are a form of collective behaviour, but those involved in the collectivity are more organized and have long-term goals. Members share a focus on working towards achieving the movement's goals. Because the group is organized it can direct the work to the members, as well as recruit and replace members and leaders if they leave. Because of these factors, social movements can gather and keep support and, unlike the more spontaneous forms of collective behaviour, achieve continuity. Except for revolutionary movements, social movements do not usually aim to change the entire social order; the aim is generally the more limited one of altering or arresting one aspect of it.

Social movements commonly go through a series of changes. The first stage involves the recognition by a number of individuals of the need for change, or for resistance to an unwanted change. A leader may emerge at this stage.

The second stage involves the development of an ideology—a clear statement of beliefs and values about what is wrong and the causes of it. Communication among members is crucial at this stage, and the mass media can help to spread the ideology and broaden the membership. In the next stage the organization is created, a more formal structure is put in place, and resources are mobilized. This will provide continuity and ensure that the social movement will be able to progress towards its goals. If the social movement achieves its goals, the movement and its ideology will become institutionalized, part of the "taken-for-granted" in society.

The two articles that follow require you to think about what is characteristic of collective behaviour and social movements. The first article describes a situation that gets some of the crowd riled up at a soccer game and is a good example of collective behaviour. The second article relates to an organization that shares common concerns with other groups dealing with environmental issues. Groups can gain collectively if they can unite around a common cause. Not only is membership broadened but press coverage is greater; the public interest thus generated and the resulting informed pressure on governments, may lead to a political solution in a democratic society.

Some Factors Governing Collective Behaviour

INTRODUCTION

Although not a major sport in North America, soccer is said to be the most widely watched sport in the world. The World Cup in soccer, played every four years, draws spectators from all the participating countries and is widely reported in the media. These matches and other sporting events that draw large crowds provide an opportunity to analyse crowd behaviour, and the ways of establishing control over crowds.

People in crowds often act in ways in which they would never act in ordinary situations. It is this dimension of crowd behaviour that fascinates sociologists. Much attention is paid to the potential for violence in a provoked and angry crowd, but crowds can also be excited and happy. Where the crowd is an audience, it can be a great stimulant to performance, as at a rock concert, theatre, or sporting event.

As you read this article, try to put yourself in the position of a spectator and observe in your mind what is going on. Think how you would have reacted, and why, and decide whether you would classify the reaction of this crowd as "collective behaviour."

Fans cry "fix" at World Cup

MADRID (CP)—West Germany scored a 1–0 victory over Austria on Friday, clinching second-round World Cup soccer berths for both teams as jeering spectators shouted fix, burned West German flags and tried to storm the field at Gijon's El Molinon Stadium.

Northern Ireland defeated host Spain 1–0 at Valencia, becoming the only unseeded team to reach the second phase. Spain also advanced from Group Five. It was the first time in 24 years Northern Ireland had qualified for the second round.

England, which qualified earlier, ousted Kuwait with a 1–0 Group Four victory in Bilbao that also assured France of a second-round spot.

The 12 teams competing in the second phase, which begins Monday after two days of rest, now are set; Group A with Poland, the Soviet Union and Belgium; Group B with England, West Germany and Spain; Group C with Italy, Brazil and defending-champion Argentina; and Group D with France, Austria and Northern Ireland.

Groups A and C will play in Barcelona, while B and D will compete in Madrid. In the second-round start Monday, Poland plays Belgium (CBC French 11 p.m. EDT) and Austria faces France (CBC English noon EDT).

Crowd incensed

The crowd watching the Group Two match between West Germany and Austria became suspicious when the game slowed down after the goal by West Germany's Horst Hrubesch, letting stand a convenient result for both sides.

The West German victory by one goal allowed both teams to advance, while a high-scoring West German victory would have eliminated Austria in favor of Algeria, which now is out of the tournament. If Austria had defeated or drawn with West Germany, Algeria would have been in and the Germans out.

After Hrubesch headed his goal off a cross from Pierre Littbarski in the 11th minute, both sides appeared content to play with the ball in midfield.

The 40,000 spectators, including hundreds of Algerian fans quickly grew impatient, angrily waving white handkerchiefs while chanting "Algeria, Algeria" and "Stop the game."

Some fans burned West German flags on stadium terraces, thousands left the stadium in disgust, while others who tried to storm the pitch were beaten back by police.

Spanish television commentators blasted both sides.

"The public who paid money to see this contest between two of the best teams in Europe are truly disillusioned with this shameful spectacle," a commentator said.

Benali Sekkal, president of the Algerian Soccer Federation called the game "scandalous and immoral."

The Austrian and West German managers both flatly denied they sought a 1–0 outcome.

The Evening Telegram, St. John's, Saturday, June 26, 1982, p. 19. With permission of The Canadian Press.

Concepts to consider:

Aggregate, collective behaviour, crowd, definition of the situation, folkways, force, group, laws, mores, social control, socialization.

QUESTIONS

1. How would you label the spectators at this soccer game—are they a group, an aggregate, a crowd, or an audience? What are the defining characteristics of the term you choose?

2. Describe anything you think would be distinctive about the spectators at this particular soccer game, compared, say, with the spectators at a local game in their home countries.

3. Under normal circumstances, is behaviour at a soccer game similar to behaviour in other situations where there is a large number of people, for example, on a crowded street, in a crowded bus, at a rock concert, or at a political rally? Describe the similarities and the differences.

4. Do norms cover the behaviour of all present at a soccer game—the teams, the spectators, the staff?

5. How do spectators learn these norms?

6. Why did some people feel that this game had been fixed? Give both the evidence, and how you imagine the crowd would come to this conclusion.

7. What did the spectators do? Explain these actions. Were such norms as existed at the start of the game suspended?

8. Explain all the sources of social control that came into play in this situation.

9. Could the spectators have become a rioting mob? What prevented it?

Ways of Gaining Support for a Protest Group

INTRODUCTION

The Queen Charlotte Islands are situated off the west coast of British Columbia, north of Vancouver Island and remote to most Canadians. The threat of exploitation of the forest resources of the Islands by commercial logging operators has aroused much protest locally among the native people and among those concerned with protecting the environment from further predation. The Island Protection Society which represents these groups needs widespread support to achieve their goal. To gain support the Society must first inform the public (the potential supporters) about an area that is unlikely to be familiar to them, and arouse their concern. The backing of environmental groups elsewhere can provide a wider base of support.

The mass media play a central role in providing publicity, but the group must first find a way of getting the media to pay attention before the public will hear the issue. The publication of a book is one way of gaining support. Involving a number of "big name" contributors captures the media's attention and in turn the public's attention and support. The group has also to compete with those who actively support resource development. They likewise can seek media attention, and thereby gain the public's attention and support for their position.

Book will focus on S. Moresby campaign

Two years ago, members from the Island Protection Society, an environmental group based in Queen Charlotte City, decided they needed a focus for their campaign to see South Moresby Island preserved as a wilderness area.

That focus was found with Islands At the Edge, a 160-page hardback to be released in mid-October.

The 10 year-old group, 12,000 members strong, is hopeful that the publication will bring further national and international attention to their cause, which is to stop resource extraction from the largely undeveloped southern island in the Queen Charlotte archipelago.

Two long-time directors of the society, John Broadhead and Thom Henley, were instrumental in initiating the project. Together they edited the book as well as writing the opening and final chapters.

"The challenge in doing the book was to communicate what South Moresby is all about. The issue has grown far beyond Island Protection Society. It's national and in some ways an international issue," says Broadhead.

Besides a core group of 500 people on the Queen Charlotte Islands committed to saving South Moresby, Broadhead says the group has heard endorsement from about 500 groups representing 400,000 people.

"There's a lot of people waiting for the book," he says.

Contributors to the book include environmentalist Jacques Cousteau, who wrote the forward, seven authors, 60 photographers and four painters.

The first section, by famed Haida artist Bill Reid, gives a cultural history, acknowledging the Haida people's need for an undamaged environment as well as a global need for unspoiled places.

The second section gives a natural history and is divided into four chapters. Within those chapters are stories on the area's vegetation, marine life, seabirds and a piece which explores the unique evolutionary path followed by some Queen Charlotte Islands creatures.

The third section of the book is the political history, which examines not only the past struggle but South Moresby's future.

Contributing painters are wildlife artist Robert Bateman, Toni Onley, Jim Willard and Takao Tanabe. Work by photographer Freeman Patterson is also featured.

The book can be pre-ordered from Douglas and McIntyre Publishers at $29.95, care of the Western Canada Wilderness Committee, 1200 Hornby Street, Vancouver, B.C. V6Z 2E2.

All royalties paid on the book will go to the Island Protection Society to help preserve South Moresby.

The Daily News, Prince Rupert, Thursday, August 16, 1984, p. 11.

Concepts to consider:

Communications, formal organization, goal, mass media, public, social movement, voluntary organization.

QUESTIONS

1. Explain what is meant by a social movement.

2. Is the Island Protection Society a social movement, the start of a social movement, or part of a social movement?

3. What concerns are the organizing group voicing?

4. What tactics are they using to mobilize support?

5. What is the long-term goal towards which they are working? How can a book serve this goal?

6. What are the goals of those who would develop the natural resources? How can they achieve their goals?

7. Apart from the groups you mentioned in answering question (6) what groups would be supporters of resource development on South Moresby? Why would they advocate development?

8. Who can stop the commercial use of the resources?

9. How will this newspaper article affect the cause of the Island Protection Society?

10. Can a group such as the Island Protection Society ensure that media coverage is positive?

FIND A CLIPPING

Find a clipping in a newspaper describing an event or a situation where a crowd has gathered. It can be any type of crowd; for example an audience at a concert, a sporting event, a religious service, a protest demonstration, or a riot.

Say what type of a crowd is described in the article. Is it a casual crowd, a conventional crowd, an expressive or an acting crowd, a riot?

Explain the situation and how the crowd is acting and reacting. What means of social control are in operation or might be imposed?

Index of Concepts

The items indexed here are those listed as "Concepts to Consider" in each section.

TO THE OWNER OF THIS BOOK:

We are interested in your reaction to **Headlining Sociology, 2/e**. Through feedback from you, we can improve this book in future editions.

1. What was your reason for using this book?

   _____ university course   _____ continuing education course

   _____ college course   _____ personal interest

2. Approximately how much of the book did you use?

   _____ ¼ _____ ½ _____ ¾ _____ all

3. What is the best aspect of the book?

4. Have you any suggestions for improvement?

5. Is there anything that should be added?

Fold here